Contents

The Open University

Block 4
Diffusion:
consumers and innovation

Dave Elliot

T307 **Innovation: designing for a sustainable future**

This publication forms part of an Open University course T307 *Innovation: designing for a sustainable future*. Details of this and other Open University courses can be obtained from the Student Registration and Enquiry Service, The Open University, PO Box 197, Milton Keynes, MK7 6BJ, United Kingdom: tel. +44 (0)870 300 60 90, email general-enquiries@open.ac.uk

Alternatively, you may visit the Open University website at http://www.open.ac.uk where you can learn more about the wide range of courses and packs offered at all levels by The Open University.

To purchase a selection of Open University course materials visit http://www.ouw.co.uk, or contact Open University Worldwide, Walton Hall, Milton Keynes MK7 6AA, United Kingdom for a brochure. tel. +44 (0)1908 858793; fax +44 (0)1908 858787; email ouw-customer-services@open.ac.uk

The Open University
Walton Hall, Milton Keynes
MK7 6AA

First published 2006. Second edition 2010.

Edited and designed by the Open University.

Typeset in India by Alden Prepress Services, Chennai.

Printed and bound in the United Kingdom by Martins the Printers Ltd.

ISBN 978 1 8487 3054 0

2.1

Introduction

This block looks at the way new products diffuse into the consumer market and at how the innovation and diffusion processes interact.

This block text has 11 sections. Each contains an introduction to relevant concepts and theories together, where appropriate, with short case studies. In line with the course's focus on the development of technologies for a sustainable future, several of the case studies are drawn from the renewable energy field. However, there are also other case studies looking at more conventional areas of technology, for example mobile phones and computer systems.

The first section introduces the idea of the diffusion of products and looks at some theories and examples of diffusion. It stresses the role of consumers, and looks at how some consumers are becoming more selective and sensitive. It introduces types of consumer response, ranging from reactive to proactive.

The second section looks at conventional passive and reactive consumer behaviour, using a case study of the diffusion of mobile phones. Section 2 also considers how businesses assess consumer needs and reactions to new products.

More proactive consumer behaviour is looked at in Sections 3, 4 and 5. Section 3 looks at how informed consumer choice can help create new markets for new products and services with a case study of green power retailing. The renewable energy theme is continued in Section 4, which has case studies of initiatives in the USA and the UK. Section 5 looks at some even more proactive examples, where some consumers have become directly involved with bottom-up, grass-roots-based innovation and diffusion initiatives in the solar energy and wind energy field.

By way of comparison with the energy examples, Section 6 looks at examples of bottom-up initiatives in the computing field and at an example of the influence of an environmental pressure group on the innovation and diffusion process, with a case study of a refrigerator.

Sections 7, 8 and 9, by contrast, look at the role of government in trying to stimulate innovation and diffusion, with a case study on the development and spread of renewable energy technologies in the UK via various market-orientated support mechanisms.

Section 10 looks back to see how some of the ideas developed in the previous sections concerning bottom-up initiatives in niche markets might help the innovation and diffusion process for new technologies like renewables. It also introduces the concept of technological regime change.

Section 11 summarises and concludes the discussion in this block text.

Aims and learning outcomes

Aims

Block 4 aims:

1   to review the factors that influence consumer uptake of new products, including environmental factors

2   to explore examples where consumers are proactive in seeking to influence the innovation and diffusion processes

3   to review the ways in which government seeks to influence the innovation and diffusion processes

4   to identify examples of niche markets and explain the idea of strategic niche management

5   to explore the extent to which diffusion of new technologies can help reduce greenhouse gas emissions and therefore contribute to a more environmentally sustainable future.

Learning outcomes

After studying Block 4 you should have achieved the following learning outcomes.

1   Knowledge and understanding

You should be able to demonstrate knowledge and understanding of:

1.1   The way in which market, environmental and economic factors influence the consumer take-up of new products.

1.2   The role of consumers in supporting new product lines, resisting unwanted options, and, on occasion, stimulating the production of, or even actually developing, desired products and services.

1.3   The difference between top-down and bottom-up approaches to innovation and diffusion and the potential role of consumers and users in aiding diffusion and innovation.

1.4   Consumer involvement with innovation and diffusion in the renewable energy sector and the problems that such activity may come up against.

1.5   The role of government in influencing the direction and effectiveness of the innovation process and the strategic development of technology, in the context of trying to move to the environmentally sustainable use of energy.

1.6   The problem of trying to pick winners in the innovation field.

1.7   The arguments for taking a longer term view in assessing the merits of new technologies and the use of learning curve analysis.

1.8   The idea of changing technological regimes and its relation to the idea of disruptive technology.

1.9   The problems and opportunities presented by niche markets for new products and services and the role that consumers and users can play in expanding them.

1.10 The role of diffusion and the part played by consumers in moving to a more sustainable approach to energy use.

2   Cognitive skills

You should be able to:

2.1 Identify in general terms the key factors likely to influence the successful diffusion of new technological developments.

2.2 Assess the relative merits of top-down and bottom-up approaches to diffusion and to the wider innovation process.

3   Key skills

You should be able to:

3.1 Analyse the relative significance of the various factors influencing diffusion.

3.2 Argue the case for and against various strategies for supporting diffusion for specific technologies or programmes.

4   Practical and professional skills

You should have gained:

4.1 Experience with writing essays and discussing arguments relating to conflicting views on strategies for diffusion.

1 Diffusion

Rudolf Diesel, inventor of the diesel engine, distinguished between two phases in technological progress. The first phase was the conception and carrying out of the idea, which he felt was a happy period of creative mental work in which technical challenges are overcome. The second phase was the introduction of the innovation, which was,

> A struggle against stupidity and envy, apathy and evil, secret opposition and open conflict of interests, a horrible period of struggle with man, a martyrdom even if success ensues.

> (Diesel, quoted in Mokyr, 1990, p.155)

Some new technologies clearly have problems in being recognised and beating off rivals. However, Diesel may have overstated the problems because many product innovations seem to translate easily to consumer or commercial markets. It is this product take-up or *diffusion* phase in the innovation process, usually seen as the final phase of the innovation process, that is the main concern of this block, how new products spread into wide use by consumers and what influences this process.

1.1 Introduction

Previous blocks have looked at how new product ideas emerge and at how the invention, design and innovation process interacts, or should interact, with the process of user need identification and market assessment. Assuming all proceeds smoothly through to the point of first introduction to the market, new technologies and new products diffuse into use through patterns of consumer uptake which are influenced by a range of factors, including not only price and performance, but also cultural factors and changes in styles and fashion.

Mobile phones initially had some limited success as a useful and prestigious gadget. This made them familiar. However, their successful diffusion only happened when the price dropped, their size reduced and performance improved, after the first wave of users started the new market and after a substantial advertising effort. For many people they have now become a fashion accessory as well as a practical device (see Figure 1).

The successful uptake of most new products is based on conventional market drivers and diffusion patterns of this type, with consumer familiarity and advertising being a key requirement. Although some new products are so transparently exciting and interesting that they take off with little need for extensive marketing, many new products are unfamiliar to potential consumers, and there is a need to create awareness of what they offer and generate demand for them.

Clearly not all new ideas and products will succeed. Even promising ideas may find it hard to get established. Some potentially valuable and technically successful new products may languish in obscurity for a while, despite marketing efforts, and some may have to await changed

Figure 1 Early mobile phone
Source: Science and Society Picture Library. By 2003 there were 50 million in use in the UK, almost one per head of population

circumstances in order for them to become successful commercially. For example, uptake may have to await crises in consumer confidence concerning existing products and a search for safer or more desirable alternatives.

Despite the power of advertising to stimulate and shape demand, consumers are not just passive receivers of new products. Not only may changes in the overall market context influence consumer behaviour, consumers also have their own changing priorities and developing needs, and these can be hard to predict.

The diffusion process is therefore not just a matter of marketing or sales promotion. Rather, attempts to manage the diffusion process involve an extension of the exploratory market research techniques that you studied in the *Markets* block, to cover the whole innovation process. Consumer feedback can affect diffusion by informing product improvements and stimulating ideas for new products.

This block accordingly looks at the diffusion of new products and systems as a process that involves a *two-way interaction* between product developers and consumers. This process determines how quickly a product or system is adopted and influences the development of products and systems longer term. So you will find that this block strays beyond diffusion to look at earlier stages in the innovation process, bringing together some of the ideas about innovation developed in earlier blocks.

This block looks at company strategies to ensure the widespread adoption of new products. But in addition I will look at the extent to which *consumers* play an active part in shaping innovation. The focus moves away from conventional innovators, people in companies seeking to develop and then market new products and systems, on to consumers, who may have their own ideas about what is needed. Although domestic consumers are the focus, it is important to remember they are not the only consumers. Most companies are consumers of products and services supplied by other companies.

As well as looking at innovators in companies and at the role of consumers, I will also look at how *governments* seek to influence the diffusion process. Governments may have views on the pattern of technological development they feel is necessary to achieve national economic and strategic priorities, including environmental targets. Environmental *pressure groups* also have an influence on both governments and companies, so I will also look at their role in shaping innovation and diffusion patterns.

In summary, this block looks at the ways in which the diffusion process occurs, how it interacts with the new product innovation process, and at how these processes are influenced by:

- companies

- consumers

- governments

- pressure groups.

1.2 Diffusion theory

Diffusion theory is a collection of concepts that attempt to explain how new ideas, products or practices are taken up into use by domestic, commercial and industrial consumers. According to Everett Rogers (1983), a leading theoretician, diffusion is 'the process by which an innovation is communicated through certain channels over time among the members of a social system' leading to its subsequent adoption into widespread use.

Diffusion can be a lengthy process. The rate of adoption is mainly influenced by the consumer's perception of the different attributes of the innovation, leading to an assessment of the overall attractiveness and desirability. As you will recall from the *Invention and innovation* block, Rogers identifies five factors that influence diffusion. He suggests the ease and rate of adoption will be increased if the product offers:

- relative advantage – in performance and/or cost terms, compared with existing products

- compatibility – with existing products, and with consumers' values and lifestyles

- complexity – by contrast, he argues that complexity is a negative attribute

- observability – seeing it in action, including seeing how others get on using it

- trialability – availability for personally checking out its merits.

In addition, *perceived risk* or *danger* in use could be added to the list as another potential disincentive.

Diffusion theory says the rate of diffusion will be affected by the decisions of both the company making and selling the product and the individuals who purchase it. Not all potential consumers will react in the same way to products. Some will buy new products earlier than others will. As you have seen in earlier blocks Rogers suggests there are five categories of adopters.

1 *Innovators*. These are the first to buy products and are willing to take the risks associated with buying an innovation.

2 *Early adopters*. This group is slightly more cautious but adopts new products quite soon after they come onto the market.

3 *Early majority*. This group buys products when they have begun to be established.

4 *Late majority*. This group buys products as the market matures.

5 *Laggards*. These consumers only buy a product when nearly everyone else has one and there is little alternative.

This classification seems fairly uncontroversial. You probably know people who rush out to buy the latest gadget and of others who resist until it can't be avoided. The resultant pattern of diffusion can be represented by a bell-shaped curve, as shown in Figure 2.

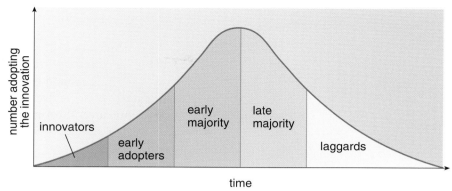

Figure 2 Rogers' diffusion curve of adopters over time

This pattern of product take-up by different groups can be traced in relation to many consumer products. The mobile phone provides a good example. The innovators and early adopters played a key role in supporting the diffusion and wider take-up of this technology. Their visible use of this new technology stimulated others to adopt mobile phones until eventually they became a must-have item for just about everyone who could afford them.

1.3   Product life cycles and s-curves

product life cycle

pattern of initial consumer uptake and subsequent decline in popularity of a new product

An understanding of diffusion patterns is clearly useful for companies concerned with maximising sales. The picture of diffusion presented by Figure 2 tends to assume that consumers simply *react* to the products offered to them, either quickly or slowly. The product-life-cycle model, which you studied in the *Markets* block, puts more emphasis on the product. It suggests that, once established in the market, products go through stages of popularity until the market for the product saturates – everyone who is likely to want one has one (Figure 3a).

In some cases products are part of a fashion cycle. After initially being popular, some products are discarded by consumers who have tired of them or have been enticed by what seems a better replacement (Figure 3b). In this portrayal consumers are seen as easily bored and needing continual injections of novelty, which enterprising innovators seek to supply. In either case, the result is a rise and then fall of sales.

1.3.1 S-curve analysis

A more sophisticated approach to product life cycles is s-curve analysis. This analysis recognises that most products undergo continued incremental innovation during their lifetime. The original product may be the result of a radical innovatory effort, but this product will be gradually refined, possibly in response to consumer reactions. Then rapid progress is made, leading to an acceleration of evolutionary development. In Figure 4 the performance is measured against time, but instead it could be measured against the money invested or the effort put into the development.

The performance continues to improve until the technology is fully developed, when the room for improvement has been exhausted and so progress slackens. If the technical performance of the device is plotted against time, then a so-called logistic growth curve results,

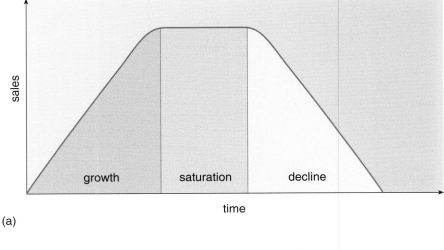

(b)

Figure 3 (a) Product life-cycle curve showing market diffusion for a product in its stages of growth, saturation and decline. (b) Fashionable or novelty product – the Hoola Hoop.

an s-shape, with an initial slow rise, followed by a rapid rise and then a flattening off (Figure 4a).

What happens after this *evolutionary* development? Usually, as the evolutionary development of the product begins to level off at the top of the s-curve, companies are likely to develop a new product as a replacement to maintain commercial success. This often involves a radical change, giving a new and better product – a *revolutionary* innovation. So a new s-curve is initiated and the process repeats. So the s-shaped curve in Figure 4(a) is seen as just the first stage of what may turn out to be generations of technological developments each with their own curve (Figure 4b).

There are usually some technological discontinuities between each stage – a jump between each curve. There may also be a period when both old and new technologies coexist and are in competition. But in general the new technology triumphs and takes over the market. Examples from the past include the transition from sail to steam in shipping. A more recent example is the switch over from propeller power to jet engines in aircraft.

More recently still, there is the transition from vinyl records to magnetic tape cassettes, and then on to compact, laser-read discs

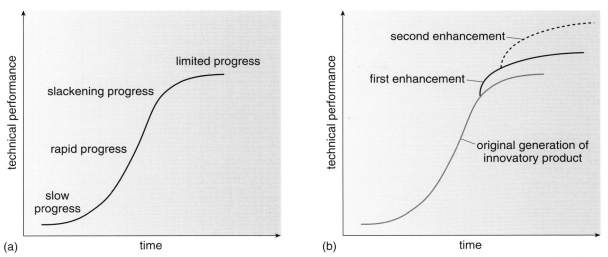

Figure 4   (a) S-curve analysis – evolutionary development. (b) S-curve analysis – revolutionary development.

(CDs), computer hard disks, and solid-state devices for sound reproduction. Figure 5 shows the declining sales of the previous technology as each new entrant took over. The pattern has continued subsequently: from the late 1990s, DVDs became a major medium, but in the early 2000s, solid-state storage and computer hard disks in portable players, with material downloaded from the internet, began to take over at least in some market sectors.

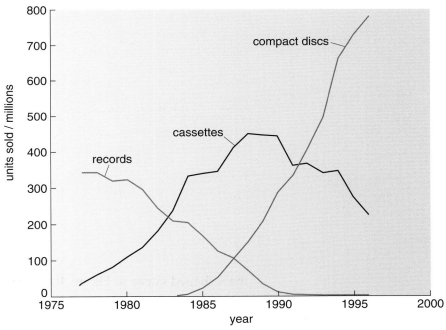

Figure 5   Switch-over from vinyl long-playing records to audio cassettes and then compact discs for recorded music media in the USA Source: data from Recording Industry Association of America, 1997

These developmental trends concern families of radical or revolutionary technologies in the same market sector, meeting roughly the same needs, although they usually do this more effectively in terms of better performance and/or better economic value. Usually the changeover to a new technology only comes about when there are perceived commercial advantages and pressures for change.

For example, when the room for further sales of the existing technology has reduced, a technological innovation offers possibilities for maintained, or ideally, increased market share.

However, the transition is by no means automatic. There are some interesting rules of thumb about what is needed before these transitions are made. One, the 10-times rule, is quite onerous: it suggests the new technology has to show an improvement that makes it 10 times better in some crucial way – only then will consumers make the change. On this basis, some analysts claim that it was not surprising that, for example, the digital audio tapes introduced in 1987 and mini-discs introduced in 1992 failed to catch on widely as the next step from standard CDs, which had been first introduced in 1982.

By contrast, the DVD, introduced in the late 1990s, quickly became ubiquitous. Early analysts (*Economist*, 1996) argued this was because the earlier devices only offered minor advantages, in terms of storage capacity or convenience, while the DVD could hold well over 10 times more information than a CD, allowing them to store films and a variety of interactive features – a big advantage over video tape. Only time will tell if DVD will survive or whether other innovations, such as Blu-ray discs or flash memory will dominate.

1.4   Consumers and diffusion

S-curve analysis is concerned mainly with general patterns of technological development. These technological changes are ultimately driven by consumer preferences, which obviously matter in terms of sales as they ultimately shape the s-curves and product life cycle curves, but specific consumer preferences have only an indirect influence on, and link back to, the technological innovation process. Market trends are identified and interpreted by companies across the market sector chiefly via their aggregated market assessments. On this model of interactions, consumers simply *react* to technological change, adopting and then becoming tired of new products.

In reality, within this diffusion process, in some cases consumers are far from passive. Certainly, consumers have increasingly become active in making *complaints* about the quality of products and services. In parallel, and more positively, consumers increasingly seem to be willing to put effort into searching for what they want. This is not to do simply with price. With a generally more affluent population, the focus is increasingly on performance and quality as well as value. As a visit to any consumer electronics retailer will confirm, consumers are becoming more selective, specialised and choosy, with new and expanding expectations of what they should be able to buy. Retailers have responded by offering wider ranges of products, as is also clear from the food retail sector.

Of course it has to be said that although the emphasis in this trend is on quality, in an affluent society it is not at the expense of quantity. The increase in consumer selectivity is embedded in what seem to be ever expanding expectations concerning the volume and quantity of goods and services consumers feel they need. It fuels consumerism – they want more *and* better. The implications of this continued growth in material expectations on environmental sustainability will be discussed in the *Consumption* block.

For the present, it should simply be noticed that not all of this enhanced consumer selectivity is related to self-interested *personal* utility concerns such as performance, quality or technical advantages, or even a desire for more things. Some consumers have adopted wider *ethical* stances in relation to what they buy and what they will not buy, and sometimes how much they will buy. In practice, only a few people opt for frugal denial, but many more are concerned about the sheer volume of their personal consumption and may seek to cut back on things they feel are frivolous or in some way undesirable.

More specifically some consumers will try to avoid products considered to be in some way ethically compromised. In particular there has been a rise in altruistic concerns relating to animal welfare, fair trading and environmental issues. For example, some will seek to avoid products that are associated with what they may view as bad environmental practices, such as the use of unsustainably managed forests or toxic chemicals.

At perhaps the most extreme, there have been consumer boycotts of all the products offered by certain companies that ethically or environmentally sensitised consumers felt were behaving inappropriately. According to research for the Co-operative Bank's Ethical Purchasing Index, in the period from 1999 to 2002, 52 per cent of UK consumers boycotted at least one product because they disapproved of the practices of the company concerned. It was estimated that £2.6 billion had been lost by firms in 2002 due to consumers switching brands on ethical grounds.

A survey in 2004 of potential consumer attitudes to companies that did not comply with the new environmental legislation requiring companies to reduce carbon dioxide emissions – introduced under the EU emissions trading scheme (EU ETS) – found that consumers would vote with their feet if companies failed to comply with this new green legislation. One in three respondents to the survey said they would switch brand allegiance on environmental grounds if a company they regularly buy goods and services from failed to comply (LogicaCMG, 2004).

As these responses suggest, there is a significant concern over environmental and ethical issues among some consumers. Moreover, consumer responses are not simply negative – some consumers will positively select products which comply with environmental legislation or which are marketed as, for example, involving fair trading with producers in developing countries, or which avoid testing on animals. Between 1999 and 2002 total sales of ethical products rose by 44 per cent, and although such products still represent a small part of the total market, this is not a trend companies can ignore.

The situation with environmental issues is similar, and companies have responded. With public concerns about climate change and damage to the ozone layer growing, products claimed to be environment friendly are now common, to such an extent that some environmental groups have issued lists of some product claims that they suspect to be 'greenwash' – in other words marketing ploys that promote a false reputation. This highlights the level of consumer awareness required to make sense of the increasingly sophisticated choices on offer – consumers have to be more aware of false or dubious claims.

Some of the products eliciting these various types of more selective and proactive consumer response do not involve innovation. The issue is often simply to do with basic trading or environmental ethics. But increasingly, as companies seek to offer wider ranges of new products to stay ahead in the marketplace, consumers are faced with *new* products that they are concerned about. Perhaps the most dramatic example is the widespread consumer resistance to genetically modified (GM) food in the UK.

The government may not have liked this particular response, but in other areas it has been keen to get more active consumer involvement, as well as the involvement of companies. In a speech to the Environment Agency's annual meeting in Birmingham in October 2004, Margaret Beckett from DEFRA challenged supermarkets 'to raise their game by only selling products that minimise environmental damage in their production and use', and argued that consumers could be more demanding when they shop.

To summarise the discussion so far, some consumers have developed ethical and environmental sensitivities that influence their purchasing decisions; some companies have responded to this new market; and the government seems keen that the public should do more, particularly in relation to selecting environmentally appropriate products.

1.5 Consumers and innovation

It is clear that consumers can influence *diffusion* by their purchasing choices, but how much impact can consumers have earlier during the development of new products? Consumer boycotts may lead to some changes in corporate policies and, if large number of consumers start making their choices from what is on offer more carefully, that can mean that markets for new products emerge.

In some cases, changes in consumer behaviour and choices do not require significant technical innovation, just a wider awareness of the claimed relative benefits of something already in existence, coupled possibly with an incentive for consumers to change their purchasing patterns. This may give suppliers an incentive to change the product mix. One example is organic food. There was a 15 per cent increase in sales between 2001 and 2002 following the various food safety scares in the UK. Subsequent health and lifestyle concerns continued to stimulate demand for organics, and supermarket chains responded to this demand.

However, in other cases, perceived or actual problems with existing products and systems can lead to wider adoption of technologies only just coming onto the market and might even lead to the development of new technologies. For example, following regular blackouts and excessive prices in California in the early 2000s, people no longer trusted the electricity grid and some had solar photovoltaic (PV) modules installed on their homes to generate their own electricity – out of necessity, to keep the power on. This stimulated the market for PV, which was a relatively new technology to most people at that time.

Of course, although widespread use is new, PV solar modules are not new technology. PV has been under development for many years, and some consumers had already adopted it. So this group of Californian PV consumers was in some senses following on from an innovator or early adopter group, those who had already adopted environmentally friendly products like solar power as a personal ethical commitment, a pioneering minority. But the newcomers have further stimulated the market for PV, and that in turn will add to the drive to develop cheaper and more marketable PV technology. This type of approach will be explored in Section 5.

Another example in the same field, which will be looked at in more detail in Section 3, is provided by the fact that by 2005 over 3 million consumers had signed up for green power retail schemes in the EU, paying their electricity suppliers to match the electricity they use with power from renewable energy sources. That in turn could stimulate the development of technology in this field.

So although the numbers of consumers involved are still relatively low, there do seem to be consumers who are willing to become proactive in various ways, including those who support the development of new technologies, and those who are seeking to move towards a more environmentally sustainable approach to consumption – in effect innovations in lifestyle. It is wise not to overstate this trend. Interest in and opportunity for involvement in changed patterns and types of consumption are limited by a range of factors, not least income levels.

In 2003, the UK's National Consumer Council (NCC) published a report entitled *green choice: what choice?*, which put consumer attitudes to 'sustainable consumption' in perspective. The NCC found from surveys carried out around the UK with people from a range of backgrounds that most consumers surveyed had a 'positive, but passive, view of sustainable consumption'. They were generally 'happy to do their bit' towards sustainable consumption, to be responsible in terms of buying green products and engaging in environmentally friendly activities like recycling, but convenience in pressured daily lives took precedence. The NCC found that,

> Low-income consumers have a much more local outlook than higher-income consumers. They also suffer most from local environmental degradation and feel powerless to improve their circumstances. Disadvantaged consumers are often shut out from making sustainable consumption choices. They have less access to facilities and lack the income to invest in more sustainable products.

(Holdsworth, 2003)

Given these variations in attitudes to sustainable consumption, it is likely that interest in a more proactive response to new technologies will be even more limited. Nevertheless, as noted above, for various reasons some consumers do adopt more challenging approaches to the products they buy and use. They may be only a minority, but companies keen to sell new products will presumably be interested in the way pioneer groups like this react. Although these ethically proactive and environmentally sensitive consumers could remain a minority, they do provide some interesting examples of a new approach to innovation and diffusion that may have wider relevance.

1.6 Consumer involvement in innovation

Consumer responses to technological innovation range from reactive to proactive. The fairly passive reactive response is usually the norm – consumers choose from what is on offer, as developed and marketed by companies, possibly with some feedback on what consumers like and want. This is the conventional form of diffusion, linked to the normal type of innovation by companies and it is a topic I will return to. But as already noted, there are also examples of more proactive approaches, and later I will look at consumers who have adopted a slightly more radical approach to what they buy.

Going one stage further, later in this block I will look at cases where consumers and users with particular interests and/or needs seek to improve the performance of products or even actually develop their own technologies themselves. This proactive response may seem at first sight to be relatively rare, but in fact it is on the increase. In 2004 the Massachusetts Institute of Technology's user innovation website even claimed that 'empirical research is finding that users rather than manufacturers are the actual developers of many or most new products and services – and that they are a major locus of innovative activity in the economy.'

This may be overstating the case – although perhaps not if you include all the software innovations being developed by users. But even in the more conventional field of physical products, what seems to be emerging is a new enthusiasm for dealing with the shortcomings of what is on offer directly, in particular in relation to specialist products and interest groups. One classic example is the mountain bike.

Case study User innovation: mountain bike

About 20 years ago a new kind of bike started appearing on British streets: the mountain bike. Where did it come from? Not from a lone inventor working in his shed, experimenting feverishly. Not from the research and development lab of a mainstream bike manufacturer.

The mountain bike came from users, especially a group of young enthusiasts in California who were frustrated that they could not ride along mountain trails on racing bikes. They put together clunky frames from traditional town bikes, gears from racing bikes, balloon tyres and motorcycle brakes.

For the first few years these bikes were made in garages, and were known as clunkers. A tiny industry emerged and by 1976 in Marin County, just north of San Francisco, there were a half a dozen small firms run by enthusiasts making bikes for their mates.

The first commercial mountain bike came out in 1982, and the big bike manufacturers piled in. By the mid eighties, 15 years after the users had developed the first mountain bike, it was a staple of the mainstream market. In 2000, mountain bikes accounted for 65 per cent of bike sales in the US, worth about $58 billion (£31.8bn). An entire product category and the lifestyle to go with it were invented not by bike manufacturers and their designers, but by the users.

(adapted from Leadbeater, 2005)

Similar examples can be found in other parts of the leisure and sports equipment field. For example, a study of consumers of outdoor sport equipment – clothing, boots, stoves and canoes – found that over 37 per cent of the sample had either developed ideas for modifications or developed new product ideas. Within this active group, 70 per cent had proposed modifications, while 30 per cent had developed new product ideas; over 40 per cent of the latter group had developed prototypes, while 30 per cent had gone on to try to market their idea. These consumers clearly had both motivation and practical experience as users to develop alternative products, and some have moved on to market them (Luthje, 2004).

In this case, some of the proactive consumers were therefore involved with innovation both in terms of developing new or modified products, and with stimulating the diffusion of the results. As you will see in some of the case studies of new products developed by proactive consumers, it is often difficult to separate out these two activities. The innovative drive often reflects a concern to develop things to meet the needs of others, whether friends, family or the wider community, so innovative product development and diffusion into use become closely linked.

As suggested above, in some cases wider environmental concerns also play a part. For example, in response to concerns about the environmental problems associated with generating electricity in Denmark in the late 1970s and early 1980s, some rural energy users, including local farmers, successfully developed new designs of wind turbine for their own use and for others around them, in local farms and villages, to use. They then set up co-operatives to manage the generators and to sell the excess electricity to the national grid. Subsequently these designs were further developed and then taken up widely around the world.

bottom-up

a development or change initiated and progressed from the grass-roots by consumers and/or users

top-down

a development or change initiated and managed from above by governments or companies, the conventional approach

There was therefore an interaction between technological innovation and market diffusion, with the initiative for both being taken initially at the grass-roots, in a bottom-up way, rather than being imposed from above, as in the conventional approach, by technical specialists and corporate interests, in a top-down way. This novel bottom-up approach is explored later.

The bottom-up approach to innovation and diffusion may not always focus on environmentally benign projects, but it is seen by some as producing better products. The approach is said to result in technologies that are shaped directly by consumer needs and users' experience. An innovation is developed by a grass-roots incremental process, with many iterative feedback loops and plenty of opportunity for trial and error.

For example, in a paper published in 2004 entitled *Harnessing the Creative Potential among Users*, which compared the ideas emerging from a group of professionals trying to improve mobile phone service with those emerging from a group of users, Per Kristensson et al said that ordinary users created significantly more original and valuable ideas than professional developers. They suggest that 'divergent thinking was facilitated through the opportunity to combine different information elements that appeared separate at the outset, such as personal needs coupled with the functionality of mobile phone service' (Kristensson et al, 2004). You will be looking at many other examples in this block.

User innovation can be a relatively slow process, but it is not expensive because it engages the commitment of enthusiasts and so can often draw on free or low cost resources. By contrast, the conventional approach to innovation, as operated by companies, seeks to be rapid and optimal in short-term economic terms – most companies cannot afford time or money to develop ideas slowly and interactively. Instead they make use of professional specialist engineers and designers, although they may augment this top-down approach with user research. However, as you saw in an earlier block some companies are already becoming aware of the benefits of enlisting users in the early stages of product development. I will look at this consumer participation and consultation approach in more detail later.

As this participative approach illustrates, a simple polarisation between top-down and bottom-up approaches misses the complexity of the real world. In reality there are varying degrees of involvement by consumers and users with the diffusion and wider innovation process, ranging from very little to a lot.

1.6.1 Consumer involvement classification

I have identified six levels of consumer involvement:

- *Level 1 passive consumers*. They just choose from what is on offer in the market place, as developed and marketed by companies in a top-down way – consumers are passive.

- *Level 2 consulted consumers*. A sample of consumers is consulted by producers on what they might want. They are given some influence on the top-down innovation process.

- *Level 3 conscientious consumers*. They apply environmental and ethical criteria to their product purchasing choices. They become more selective.

- *Level 4 specialist consumers*. They have special interests and create new markets with their purchasing choices. They influence the market in a bottom-up way.

- *Level 5 developer consumers*. They develop new or modified products to meet their needs or concerns. They become more proactive in a bottom-up way in terms of technological innovation, and sometimes operate in niche markets.

- *Level 6 consumer innovators*. Consumer initiatives lead to success and diffusion. The products transcend the niche markets created by these proactive consumers, and these products and the enterprises that have created them may become part of the mainstream. These consumers change the market and the products, and these changes may become part of the new order.

At each successive level in this list, the influence of *businesses* on innovation and diffusion decreases, as *consumer* influence and involvement increases. However, in all categories, business involvement is still strong and ultimately, at level 6, any successful products emerging from the bottom-up process are likely to be taken up by conventional companies.

The majority of consumer behaviour is at level 1 in the list – this is the base line. As the examples in this block illustrate, subsequent categories in this list involve progressively fewer people. While significant numbers may influence *diffusion* by changing their purchasing patterns in line with their ethical or environmental concerns, only a minority will usually have the motivation, time or resources to be proactive in terms of developing new products (level 5). Certainly, in many sectors, successful independent innovation by people outside of companies is relatively rare, although it has to be remembered that in terms of numbers involved, even in the corporate context, only a relatively few people (those in specialist R&D groups and new product development teams) are directly involved with innovation.

At level 6 the situation changes. Greater numbers of people are involved as the product diffuses into the niche market and then later as the new idea spreads and is taken up widely. Once the product has been adopted by the mainstream, diffusion takes place like any other corporate product, and consumer involvement reverts to level 1.

The levels of consumer involvement shown above apply to individual consumers and small grass-roots user groups. However, these are not the only sources of external influence on the rate of technological development and diffusion. Consumers can also be part of wider consumer organisations and environmental pressure groups. Such groups can have significant impacts on company plans and new product developments through the lobbying power and public influence of large numbers of members. For example, green groups may oppose nuclear power and support solar power. Clearly, given the involvement of grass-roots activists, this is a bottom-up approach, although some pressure groups have national and international roles and can be major players in the high-level political processes.

Businesses are therefore not the only focus for pressure group lobbying. Governments are also targeted, because they have ultimate responsibility for regulating the activities of businesses and have their own policies on technological development. Indeed, governments often seek to direct the development and deployment of technologies based on their view of national strategic priorities and are often themselves major players in terms of innovation in some sectors, such as defence-related technologies.

Governments influence the mix of products and systems in ways often beyond the control of consumers, through regulation, taxes and other policy mechanisms. They seek to stimulate the development and diffusion of selected technologies in line with wider national or international strategic priorities. For example, based on environmental policy, governments may seek to phase out the use of coal for electricity generation and to back wind, wave or tidal power. Clearly this sort of influence involves a top-down approach, although one moderated by democratic processes.

Pressure groups and government present consumers with additional ways of influencing innovation. For pressure groups this may be through active involvement in the group; for government this may only be through the ballot box or through asking questions of elected members.

However, in this block you will consider the involvement of government and pressure groups separately from that of the individual consumer as these two groups represent additional ways in which business activities are challenged, modified or regulated to influence innovation.

In the subsequent sections of this block you will look at the various levels of consumer, government and pressure group involvement in innovation through a series of case studies.

Be aware that the case studies I use often not only illustrate diffusion patterns based on consumption but also look at the influence of consumers on the whole innovation process. As was suggested earlier, the interactions between the development of new products and consumer attitudes and responses to technology are important. That is why, in this block, you will look at both ends of the innovation process – the early phase of product development as well as the final phase of product diffusion.

1.7 Technological selection

A common theme in all of the levels of consumer involvement, business and government responses is *selection*. Even the most passive consumer has to select from what is on offer. In his book *Enabling Innovation*, Boru Douthwaite describes innovation as involving a Darwinian process of selection. New ideas are tested, tried and adopted only if they are seen as valuable by consumers (Douthwaite, 2002a).

Douthwaite suggests the three stages of natural selection as outlined by Charles Darwin also apply to technological innovation. In the biological version, natural selection is held to involve the following stages:

1   *Novelty generation.* Because of random genetic mutations and sexual recombination of different genetic material, significant differences between individual members of a species crop up from time to time.

2   *Selection.* This is the mechanism that retains random changes that turn out to be beneficial to the species because they enable those possessing the trait to achieve better survival and breeding rates. It also rejects harmful changes.

3   *Diffusion and promulgation.* These are the mechanisms by which the beneficial differences are spread to other areas.

By contrast, in natural selection for technology, the first stage of selection, novelty generation occurs because of conscious human effort and imagination, in response to need or curiosity. This is not a random event or accident as happens in nature, although chance can sometimes play a role in sparking ideas. The selection of technologies is made not only on technical fitness and economic consideration, but also on the basis of social values and cultural perceptions of what is appropriate.

That, arguably, makes the technological selection process different from what happens in nature – choosing technology is a conscious human process.

Douthwaite claims that for successful innovation this human process of choice is crucial and should be enhanced. He argues that in the case of human-generated technologies selection can and should occur at each stage of innovation. Moreover, he says, there should be more feedback between the stages, especially between the first stage (novelty generation – invention) and the last (diffusion).

He notes that in the conventional view of the innovation process the starting point is when inventors decide which line to follow, and at the other end of the process consumers decide which product to buy from what is offered to them. The consumers have no direct influence over the choice of which product is developed. However, as you may recall from the *Invention and innovation* block, Douthwaite argues this segmented approach to choice and innovation, where products are simply tossed 'over the wall' to consumers, is not the only option. He argues that the involvement of consumers early on in the process can lead to more appropriate technological developments that will in turn aid diffusion.

The case studies that follow should help you to assess whether he is right, and whether there is a better process than natural selection.

SAQ 1

Proactive consumers are a minority, a small group of altruistic enthusiasts with special interests of little significance to mainstream markets. So why bother to consider this marginal group in any detail?

Key points of Section 1

- Diffusion is the final stage of the innovation process, and is concerned with the take-up of new products by consumers.

- The rate of diffusion at any one time depends on how consumers react to new products. Some will adopt them quickly, most others will take their time, and a few will remain hesitant until there is no other option.

- New products usually go through a cycle of initial popularity and sales followed by decline. Some products are incrementally improved until they are replaced by newer, better products, and the cycle may then repeat.

- In the conventional depictions of consumer responses to products, consumers are seen as passive – simply selecting from what is on offer. However, some consumers are becoming more selective and some are concerned about ethical, social and environmental issues and are adjusting their purchasing choices accordingly.

- Consumers with special needs or concerns may become more proactive and seek out, support or even develop radically new products. This is a shift from passive involvement to proactive innovation, which may lead to diffusion of the resulting product.

- A bottom-up grass-roots approach to innovation may offer some advantages over a top-down approach, by ensuring involvement of users in both product development and diffusion.

The key points for Section 1 meet learning outcomes 1.1, 1.2 and 1.3.

2 Conventional consumer involvement

2.1 Passive consumer

The most obvious type of consumer response, and the first level of involvement, is to simply choose from what is on offer in the market place. This is what happens in the case of most consumer products and it is the basis for most of the marketing and promotion approaches adopted by most businesses. As was discussed in the *Markets* block, whether products succeed or fail depends on whether the right marketing mix has been adopted. This will influence the level of response from consumers.

The case study below looks at the rapid diffusion of mobile phones. The case provides a classic example of a successful product and marketing mix, and an illustration of the adopter responses outlined by Rogers – indeed Rogers included a short case study of mobile phones (aka cell phones) in the USA in the fourth edition of his classical book *The Diffusion of Innovations* (1995). He says that 'cellular phones have an almost ideal set of perceived attributes, and this is undoubtedly one reason for the innovation's very rapid rate of adoption in the US'. As you will see, since 1995 the rate of adoption has accelerated and extended worldwide.

2.2 Brief history of mobile phone innovation and diffusion

Radio telephones of various types have been available since the 1940s, but they were expensive, and used special frequencies of normal wireless channels that were limited in number. They also needed large aerials, which meant their main market was for use in vehicles. Military walkie-talkies and police radios of various kinds provided more portable point-to-point radio contact over limited ranges, and the cheaper multichannel citizens' band (CB) radio came into widespread use, initially in the USA in the late 1970s and in the early 1980s in the UK. But the CB sets were still quite bulky and they did not provide secure person-to-person communication – everyone in the albeit relatively limited range and on the same channel could listen in.

The idea of deploying large numbers of small, relatively short-range transmitters and receivers to create a network of interlinked zones or cells, and thereby provide a personal two-way link for individual users, was first mooted in 1947 by researchers at the Bell Labs in the USA. However, it was not taken up until the 1970s, by which time advances in microelectronics, and later digital techniques, made it possible to have smaller handsets. Even so, the first mobile phones were still bulky (Figure 6). They were also expensive. Rogers reports that initially they were a perk for executives, costing around $3000 each in 1983. But once they emerged and the market started building, technical progress and miniaturisation was rapid, and costs fell.

By the late 1990s the mobile phone had arrived centre stage and, with occasional dips, the global market has continued to expand (Figure 7). By 2002, globally, the number of mobile subscribers had overtaken the number of fixed-line subscribers, and expansion has continued. Box 1 provides a historical summary of the diffusion process.

(a)   (b)

Figure 6 Mobile phone development: (a) the first portable units were big and heavy, and few were as glamorous as this one made by Spectrum Cellular Corporation Source: www.privateline.com; **(b) the first mobile phone in the hand of Martin Cooper, who is widely credited as being the father of the mobile phone (aka cell phone)** Source: courtesy of Dr Martin Cooper, ArrayComm

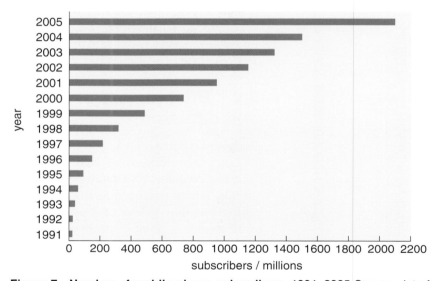

Figure 7 Number of mobile phone subscribers, 1991–2005 Source: data from International Telecommunication Union and Cellular Online

---

Box 1 Mobile phone diffusion: landmark dates

1973 Martin Cooper, former general manager for the systems division at Motorola, is usually considered the inventor of the first portable handset and was the first person to make a call on a mobile phone (aka cell phone). He set up a base station in New York with the first working prototype phone, the Motorola DynaTAC.

1977 Mobile phones went public in the USA. Public mobile phone testing began. The city of Chicago was where the first trials began with 2000 customers, and eventually other phone trials appeared in the Washington DC and Baltimore areas.

1979 Japan began testing a mobile phone service.

1982 Cellnet (BT with Securicor) and Vodafone (Racal with Minicom) were awarded the UK's first mobile phone licences.

1985 The UK's first ever commercial mobile phone call, using a Vodafone handset.

1988	Cellnet connects its ten-thousandth customer.
1990	Vodafone customer base reaches 500 000.
1993	Mercury One 2 One launched. Pay-as-you-go contracts are offered.
1994	Orange launched. One 2 One connects ten-thousandth UK customer.
1994	Cellnet connects 1 millionth UK customer.
1995	Japan has nearly 9 million subscribers, about 7% of the population.
1998	One 2 One connects millionth UK customer.
1999	Nokia launches the 3210 design, sometimes seen as the iconic Ford Model T of mobile phones. The Orange network promotes it heavily. Nokia, based in Finland, goes on to capture 34% of the mobile handset market.
2000	Almost 50% of UK population has a mobile phone.
2001	More than 1000 million people have mobile phones globally, led by Japan and Europe.
2002	Cellnet (reconfigured as O$_2$) has 11 million UK customers. New technologies emerge, such as WAP (web-enabled) and 3G (third generation, faster data flow, video-enabled). Over 50% of the 70 million mobile phone subscribers in Japan have internet access handsets. China takes the lead globally with 160 million mobile phone subscribers – 12% of its population.
2003	Around 50 million mobile phones are in use in the UK – equal to roughly one per person. Globally there are over 1300 million mobile phone subscribers.
2004	After a slow start, 3G subscriptions reach 1 million in the UK.
2005	The UK National Radiological Protection Board suggests that because of possible health risks mobile phones should not be used by young children. A phone aimed at this market is withdrawn by the manufacturers.
	Global phone subscriptions reach about 2 billion.

For an interesting account of the history of mobile phones, see Agar (2003). For statistics on mobile phone usage see the website of the International Telecommunication Union at **www.itu.int/home**.

2.3   Mobile phone diffusion in the UK

Initially, in the late 1980s and early 1990s, mobile phones were expensive and were often seen, with envy in some cases, as a status product for what were then called young, upwardly mobile professionals (yuppies). Certainly owners were often ostentatious about using their phones in public, and this helped build demand – as well as resentment.

The market gradually expanded and prices fell in a two-way interaction. However, although the handsets may have been cheaper, initially the connection, line rental and call charges were often high. In some cases handsets were given away free or at low cost to attract customers, who then were faced with large bills when they came to use them. It was not until new, more attractive subscription schemes emerged, including plug-in pre-payment cards, that large numbers of people signed up. That coincided with major advertising campaigns in print and other media.

In the 2000s, manufacturers introduced advanced features, like WAP (web-enabled phones), and developments continue in an effort to expand the market. However, text messaging and personalised ring tones have so far proved to be the most popular aspects. The popularity of texting seems to be in part because it is a cheap way to communicate – some companies had provided it as a free bonus service, but had not expected it to be widely used.

More high-tech additions have also proved popular, for example the addition of imaging and video facilities, although 3G, the promised third generation revolution, was slower to take off than expected. But with teenagers becoming innovators and or early adopters in Rogers' terms, the boom in mobile phones and their continued technological development seems unstoppable – they are seen as one of the most successful new products to have emerged in recent years.

Overall, the benefits of mobile phones are clear, and they have had an impact not only in terms of business use, but also on lifestyles in general, allowing busy people to stay in contact with family and friends. In his 1995 update, Rogers notes that 'one of the main benefits of the cellular telephone is that it saves an estimated two hours per week in avoiding missed appointments and delayed schedules, and improves time management'.

One downside has been concern about the health risk from exposure to microwave radiation. This has led some to use hands-free earpiece extensions and it was another reason why hand-held texting was popular. The use of mobile phones while driving has been another source of hazard, but was made illegal in the UK in 2003. Occasional lack of connectivity due to poor reception in marginal areas along with the need for frequent battery charging has made the phones less than 100 per cent reliable in emergencies. Nevertheless, having a mobile phone is seen as providing an important safeguard for anyone who needs to summon help urgently.

2.4 Diffusion around the world

The diffusion of mobile phones initially spread rapidly in the industrialised countries – in Europe, the USA and especially Japan, where as Box 1 illustrates, uptake was dramatic. South Korea also saw rapid growth in the use of mobile phones. Interestingly there are cultural differences in how such devices are perceived, and the diffusion of 3G phones was much faster in Asia than in the EU or the USA.

Perhaps less predictably, sales have also begun to expand rapidly in the developing world. In the case of China, which is industrialising rapidly, this is understandable. By 2002 China had become the largest user of mobile phones in the world, with 160 million subscribers, more than the number of users in the USA at that time. However, this numerical lead was due to China's large population – only just over 12 per cent of population had mobile phones in 2002 compared with almost 38 per cent of Americans. But growth in the Chinese market has been rapid. By 2003 over 16 per cent of the population had mobile phones, with market penetration in some areas being much higher – for example, by 2003 nearly 85 per cent of Hong Kong residents had mobile phones.

Expansion is also under way in less developed countries, particularly in Africa, where by 2004 around 60 million people were using mobile phones. The provision of effective communications is seen as a key to economic development, not least in terms of providing access to the power of the internet. But the large distances between centres of population and the diffuse distribution of the rest of the population in Africa have presented problems for conventional landline communication. By 2004 only 27 million people in Africa had conventional landline telephones – 2.8 per cent of the population.

Radiotelephony is an obvious answer. Although expensive, satellite phones have become quite widely used, mobile phone networks have also spread rapidly. In the five years up to 2004, mobile phone use in Africa expanded by 65 per cent, twice the global average. The geographical coverage was still patchy, with about half the population being out of range of cellular networks. By 2004 only around 6 per cent of the population actually had mobile phones. But the potential for further expansion is enormous. That is seen as crucial for the region in terms not just of economic development but also of social development.

In this context, mobile phones and the associated information networks could be seen as a vital tool for economic modernisation, education and social change. So the impetus for diffusion may not always be just conventional consumer needs – it can also involve wider social concerns. For example, in 2003 a mobile phone network was launched in rural Uganda, designed for use by women in remote areas of the country. The plan was to have a loan scheme, and use car batteries to charge the phones. One of the aims was to support local social and economic development by linking up with the projects that rural women had created (Sustainable Africa, 2002).

Exercise 1   Responses to innovation of mobile phones

Drawing on Box 1 and your own experience, analyse consumer responses to mobile phones once they came on the market in the UK, in terms of the six key characteristics of innovations discussed earlier – relative advantage, observability, complexity, trialability, compatibility, and risk. You may recall that earlier in the course you were asked to carry out a similar exercise based on Rogers' categories. Notice, however, that in this block an extra characteristic – risk – has been added to Rogers' five characteristics. This block has also explored the technological development and market take-up history of mobile phones in a little more detail.

Discussion

Once consumers were familiar with what they could offer, mobile phones had obvious attractions in terms of utility, and as the market grew, device performance improved and costs fell. So not only were there clear relative advantages over fixed-line telephones and earlier mobile communication technologies in terms of performance and function, but also these advantages increased with time.

Observability has proved to be a key to the success of mobile phones – they are available in a variety of often attractive designs and have become ubiquitous, and, for good or ill, widely and visibly used in public.

Trialability too is relatively straightforward – you can borrow a friend's phone – as is complexity, in terms of learning how to use them, at least for some people. The basic technique is similar to conventional phones, which have also undergone technical upgrades, although the increasingly small size of mobiles and their ever more advanced features can make using them daunting to novices.

In terms of compatibility with existing technologies, they connect to the existing phone system, so there was no need to reach a critical mass of users before they became viable, but whether they are compatible with users' values and lifestyles is a matter of debate – some welcome the freedom mobile phones give, others hate their intrusiveness.

But overall, there are clearly many strongly positive factors, although the health risk factor remains an unknown. Another risk factor – unexpectedly high bills and expensive connection fees – was initially a significant problem for many users, as was occasional lack of connectivity.

Exercise 2   Diffusion of mobile phones

Analyse the diffusion of mobile phones using Rogers' classification of types of adopter: innovators, early adopters, and so on.

Discussion

Given the relatively high cost of the early phones, the 'innovators' were usually wealthy business people. The ostentatious display of these items may have stimulated others to become early adopters, but take-up by the early majority had to await cheaper phones and less expensive billing arrangements. It was probably the continued reduction in costs and the expansion of advertising that attracted the late majority, which included the adoption of mobile phones by teenagers.

The market was continually stimulated by new technological improvements, and to some extent that has involved some recycling through the same pattern, the more advanced features (WAP, videophones, 3G) have attracted 'innovators' including increasing numbers of teenagers, and so the cycle repeats. The laggards are a minority who presumably either dislike the invasiveness of mobile phones, or who are unwilling or unable to face the complexity they feel is involved in operating and maintaining them. There will also of course be a group who cannot afford them.

Exercise 3   Success of mobile phones

Analyse the success of the mobile phone in terms of the 4 Ps – product, promotion, price, place – as discussed in the *Markets* block.

Discussion

The mobile phone is a unique and inventive product. As you have seen, innovation has clearly been critical for its successful diffusion. The basic technology is innovative and there have been continual quite radical developments, the addition of digital cameras, video cameras and Web access. Design has also played a major role – with a wide range of new configurations, shapes, colours and sizes emerging. In addition marketing and promotion has played a key role, both initially and then subsequently alerting potential consumers to the new features of the latest products.

Price was initially a problem, but rapid cost-cutting and technological development, combined with new billing arrangements, have made mobile phones affordable to most people in the industrialised world, and also to many elsewhere. Indeed, as you saw, sales in some developing countries have been quite dramatic.

In terms of place, the obvious utility and visibility of mobile phones has made them relatively easy to sell, with supermarket chains as well as specialist electronics retailers all vying for customers.

2.5   Consumer reactions to new products

Although its utility could rapidly be understood, the mobile phone was a more or less completely new concept to most consumers. Marketing and promotion, along with good design and rapid innovation, played a major role in its successful diffusion, and this success has continued as newer models have emerged.

However, simply trying to promote new products in the hope they will sell may not be sufficient for successful diffusion in every case. With novel products of this type increasingly being developed, and consumers becoming more choosy, the need for more sophisticated market research has grown. As was discussed in the *Markets* block, businesses increasingly try to find out how consumers will respond to new products, and what new products they might like.

Some of the information that might be gained from improved consumer consultation might be relatively trivial, although nevertheless important for marketing purposes and hence for sales. It is interesting, for example in the case of mobile phones, how consumers decided that texting and personalised ring tones were important facilities – this had not been expected by manufacturers. However, there might be more significant information on consumer preferences that could influence the type of products produced.

2.6   Consulted consumer

The second level of consumer involvement is a level at which the consumer is consulted by companies developing new products.

In the *Markets* block you have seen how some companies are now adopting a user-centred approach to design, both to identify potential areas for new product development and to better understand user needs in relation to specific products. The user-centred design approach is characterised by carrying out in-depth, observational research with a small number of people to find problems and opportunities for new product design. Companies such as Philips Design and IDEO see this approach as a way of developing successful products that are quickly diffused into the marketplace.

In a user-centred design approach the influence of the consumer will only be as wide or as narrow as the given brief. For example, young people brought in to comment on a well-developed phone design may influence the design of detailing and functionality but are less likely to provoke designers into having a complete rethink of the phone concept. However, when used as part of strategic design, such as the Presence Project (see the *Markets* block) and its design of communication systems in Biljmer, the consumers' responses may strongly influence the designers and lead them into unexpected and novel territory.

Case study | Aqualisa Quartz shower

In 1998 a small British shower manufacturer, Aqualisa, prototyped an innovative design of shower that has subsequently gone on to become a successful product. The first ideas for the Quartz shower were conceived several years earlier and had been developed subsequently by Aqualisa working in conjunction with the renowned design agency Seymour Powell. However, the product was not developed until the company sensed the market might be prepared to pay for a high-cost, high-quality shower.

In 1998 the prototype was created and Aqualisa carried out user research to see how its new product might be received. The method the company chose was to create a 'safe house' containing a shower room in which people could be observed taking a shower as well as being interviewed about their experience. This user-centred approach led to some minor modifications of the design, though it largely confirmed that the design team had instinctively understood user needs.

However, Aqualisa recognised that retailers and plumbers would also play an important part in the successful diffusion of their product. The company conducted extensive research with retailers and plumbers to identify the main issues surrounding shower purchasers. This consultation showed the main problem to be the complexity of shower installation and the time required – installation typically taking two days and often involving more than one person.

The outcome was the design of an innovative shower system in which the mixing of water to the required temperature occurred outside the shower, enabling this component to be located under the bath, in the loft or in any other convenient site. With the mixing component located elsewhere the shower can be fitted by surface mounting rather than recessing – unless recessing is preferred. This significantly reduces the amount of time taken in installation.

The company also created a highly graphic installation manual using photographs, rather than text, to illustrate each step of the process.

The results of these innovations are that it is possible to install a Quartz shower in two hours, and the high cost of the product is offset by the significantly reduced installation cost.

The Aqualisa Quartz was slow to diffuse at first, attributed mainly to reluctance from the plumbing industry to recommend an unknown product. However, small independent retailers were instrumental in ensuring the growing success of the product and by 2002 the Quartz had become the company's best-selling product (Figure 8).

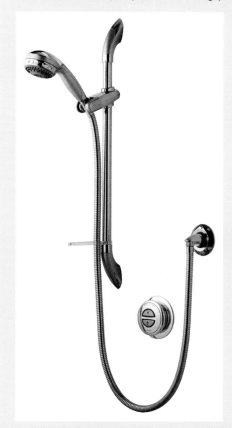

Figure 8   Aqualisa Quartz shower Source: Aqualisa

This level of consumer involvement in innovation offers the consumer a more active role in the process of product development; however, the initiative for change in such a situation still has to come from the manufacturer.

Even manufacturers who simply watch trends, or more adventurously, carry out blue-sky thinking (strategic proposals about as-yet unfeasible ideas) should follow through any ideas that come about because of user research and consultation.

Customer and user requirements are even more influential when the 'consumer' is a company, particularly if that company has commissioned a product. In such a case the detailed needs and requirements of the consumer will be considered and the two companies will negotiate the product specification. For large or innovative projects, there is likely to be a continuing process of discussion on adjustment and modifications as the project unfolds.

The next section looks at how consumers can influence commercial success and the nature of the product offered through their purchasing choices. For example they may buy energy-efficient domestic equipment and sign up to green-power retail schemes that rely on consumers deciding to switch to using power from renewable energy sources.

Key points of Section 2

- Most consumers simply choose from what is on offer, with promotion and marketing activities providing an impetus, but innovation and good design are also obviously important.

- Mobile phones provide a good example of how consumers respond to new products, in line with the classifications of types of adopters and product characteristics provided by Rogers.

- The success of the mobile phone owes much to creative design and continual innovation, as well as benefiting from marketing efforts.

- While some products seem almost to sell themselves, for the successful diffusion of many other new products there may also be a need to assess potential consumer reactions more effectively.

- Companies are increasingly attempting to assess user needs and their reactions to proposed products.

- User-centred design techniques can influence product designs, leading to a greater chance of commercial success.

- The consumer may be an individual or an organisation, in which case there may be a high degree of interaction.

- Successful diffusion depends on the attitudes of people at all points of the distribution chain.

The key points for Section 2 meet learning outcome 1.1.

3 Consumer choice and new energy technologies

3.1 Conscientious consumer

This section looks at the third level of consumer involvement in which consumers reflect ethical and environmental commitments in their purchasing decisions and so begin to take a more proactive role influencing the way technology is developed and which technologies are developed.

There is no shortage of examples of new green or ethical consumer products that consumers can decide to buy. The *Products* block looked at examples of how some of these new green products have been developed. A common feature in many of them is attention to energy use. This is not surprising because energy generation from the combustion of fossil fuels is probably the largest single source of environmental problems, most obviously in the case of climate change.

Growing awareness of these issues seems to be having an impact not only on people's views about how energy is generated, but also on their attitudes towards the price of energy. In 2002, as part of a review of UK energy policy, the Department of Trade and Industry (DTI) sought the opinions of people drawn from a cross-section of the UK in a consultation process that consisted of focus groups, workshops and web-based questionnaires. For example, the DTI invited members of the public to events in Birmingham, London, Cardiff and Glasgow. Two of the key findings of all the stages of the consultation process were as follows:

- Strong interest was shown in the environmental aspects of energy policy. The need to address pollution and climate change featured prominently in discussions on energy policy.

- There was firm support for energy efficiency and renewable forms of energy; many respondents were concerned that by focusing on lower energy prices the government might be sending the wrong signal about using energy efficiently.

The consultation showed that low prices were not the main concern of the consumers who were consulted. Environmental concerns have become important to an increasing number of people in the UK. Of course commitments made in the abstract may not be acted on in practice. This section looks at the extent to which consumers have opted for more environmentally friendly ways of obtaining and using energy, focusing on energy use in the home and on electricity in particular.

3.2 Energy efficiency and renewable energy

The most obvious way for consumers to reduce the environmental impact of domestic energy use is by investing in basic energy efficiency measures, such as loft insulation, double-glazing and cavity wall insulation. They can also improve the efficiency with which they use gas for space and water heating by installing condensing gas central heating boilers. In addition, consumers can reduce their use of electricity by buying energy efficient electrical and electronic equipment such as fridges, washing machines, computers, TV sets, video and DVD players and so on, and by replacing conventional light bulbs with more efficient compact fluorescent lamps. In most cases, it is relatively easy for consumers to switch over to more efficient devices of this sort – there are many products available on the market, and using them has the attraction of lowering running costs. (Box 2 has an overview of progress between the 1970s and early 2000s.)

Box 2 Energy efficiency

In the UK there have been a number of government-led campaigns, policies and programmes designed to stimulate the uptake of energy-efficiency measures. These have included grants to meet the cost of installing insulation and the reduction of valued-added tax on some energy-efficient products and materials. These inducements have met with varying degrees of success. For example, whereas in 1976 only around 38 per cent of UK houses had loft insulation, by 2000 this had risen to over 72 per cent or 17.5 million of the 24.3 million UK households – not all households have loft access. Between 1970 and 2000, insulation measures like this, coupled with the adoption of more energy efficient heating appliances, cut overall UK domestic energy demand for heating by about 48 per cent from what it would have otherwise been. Insulation made a slightly larger contribution to this reduction than improvements in heating appliances.

However, the overall use of energy for space heating in the UK still rose by 24 per cent between 1970 and 2000, partly because there were increasing numbers of households, but also because there was widespread adoption of central heating systems and higher general room temperatures.

Space heating is the largest single element of domestic energy use. By 2000, it accounted for around 58 per cent of the total. But other uses of energy in the home have also expanded. For example, between 1970 and 2000 energy use for domestic water heating rose by 15 per cent and energy use for lighting and appliances increased by a massive 157 per cent, despite a significant take-up of energy efficient lamps. Market penetration of compact fluorescent lamps (CFLs) increased from 7 per cent of all households in 1992 to 23 per cent in 1997 when cheaper CFLs became available. Their widespread availability meant sales continued to increase throughout the 2000s.

However, as can be seen, the take-up of energy efficiency measures and devices did not keep pace with the rise in energy demand. As a result, overall domestic energy use rose by a third between 1970 and 2000 and continued to rise thereafter, despite increasing levels of support for energy efficiency measures. For example, domestic use of electricity increased by 1.6 per cent between 2003 and 2004, while gas consumption in the domestic sector rose by 3.3 per cent in 2004.

Diffusion problems

One of the problems for the diffusion of energy efficiency measures is that energy is still relatively cheap, so there is no major financial incentive to cut back on using it as the cash savings will be relatively low. It may take a long time to pay back the initial capital outlay for new appliances, and modern career and employment patterns mean that people move home more often, and may not be able to benefit from investment in systems with long payback times.

Some environmentally orientated consumers will adopt energy efficiency measures even if there is only a small saving or even no saving, but unless energy prices increase significantly or concerns about climate change begin to change consumer behaviour significantly, overall the prospects for making large energy savings and consequent emissions reductions in this sector via efficiency measures do not seem great.

This view is further strengthened by another problem – the so-called rebound effect. Even assuming the wide-scale diffusion of energy efficiency measures is successful, it may not lead to significant reductions in emissions, because at least some of the money saved when consumers invest in energy efficient domestic measures is likely to be spent on extra energy intensive goods and services. The obvious examples are buying a dishwasher or tumble dryer or going on a holiday abroad by jet plane.

So the initial energy saving, and the environmental benefits that implies, may be undermined. The net energy used by the household may not fall significantly, and the carbon dioxide emissions associated with burning fossil fuels to generate the electricity it uses may therefore not be reduced substantially. You will be looking at the rebound effect in more detail in the *Consumption* block.

As Box 2 illustrates, although some gains have been made, there are limits to what can be achieved by consumers in terms of reducing emissions through adopting technical measures to improve energy efficiency. Certainly, so far, savings from energy efficiency improvements are not keeping up with increases in demand for energy – the gains are being wiped out. Moreover, prospects for increased technical efficiency improvements do not look too good. When all the easy and cheap energy efficiency options have been exhausted ('picked all the low-hanging fruit'), the cost of making further savings is likely to rise.

renewable energy
an energy source, such as the sun, that won't be exhausted in the foreseeable future and won't generate pollutants

So what about the more radical approach of using renewable energy? After all, that can eliminate emissions. Not many consumers will be able or willing to install, for example, wind or solar technologies directly in their homes. However, there is the option of contracting into green power schemes run by energy companies who, in effect, offer to generate power from renewable energy sources on behalf of consumers.

Despite the problems facing energy efficiency outlined above, do not think that it is irrelevant or that switching to green power is the only solution. Energy efficiency is a crucial part of any attempt to move towards reduced emissions and there is scope for continued innovation in the development of new energy saving techniques and systems, as well as behavioural and lifestyle changes that could cut energy demand dramatically. The *Consumption* block discusses this topic further.

However, if the threat of climate change is to be reduced there will be a need for both increased efficiency of energy use *and* a switch over to non-fossil-fuel energy sources like renewables. Certainly energy efficiency measures and green power schemes should not be seen as mutually exclusive alternatives. Indeed, they can and should be mutually reinforcing. For example, if consumers use the cash saved from domestic energy efficiency measures to buy in green power, they can avoid the rebound effect (see Box 2) – and also offset the extra cost of renewable energy. Equally, it makes sense to deal with energy losses in houses and so on before investing in often more expensive renewable energy supplies, and if energy use can be reduced it becomes easier to meet it from renewable sources.

3.3   Green power retailing

A range of green power schemes are on offer in the UK for contracting with retailers to pay for green power produced by commercial generators. Such schemes have the merit of offering the consumer an easy way to 'go green' – all they have to do is change suppliers or arrange a new contract with their existing supplier, which usually involves a phone call, or a short session on the internet.

The green power market emerged as part of a wider process of UK electricity market liberalisation. From May 1999 this meant that consumers could choose to make a contract for their electricity supply with any electricity supply company, not just their local area supply company. Subsequently, the regional electricity companies, which had emerged from the privatisation of the regional electricity boards in 1990, introduced a range of supply deals to try to compete in the new power market. Most of them included green power schemes of various sorts.

The main aim of the companies, at least initially, seems to have been customer retention – they did not want other companies poaching any customers, so each had to have their own green schemes. So the focus of their advertising was their existing customers. However, there was also initially a limited amount of general advertising in the print media that appeared to be aimed at trying to establish the green credentials of the companies concerned.

Apart from these initial campaigns, the regional electricity companies mostly did not promote the schemes heavily, as the green power market was seen as rather marginal to their main business. They were also uncertain what consumer response would be. Early on there was also not much green power available for the regional electricity companies to buy, so they were cautious about promoting the schemes too widely. In contrast some small independent supply companies emerged, specialising in retailing green power from local generators, and they promoted the idea quite strongly.

The marketing emphasis for green power overall has been on consumers likely to have environmental concerns, with the brand names being chosen accordingly. So one of the first schemes was called Green Electron, another was called Evergreen, and subsequently there was Ecotricity, the latter being offered by an independent supply company. Evidently aiming for an even wider appeal, another independent company chose the name Good Energy for its scheme.

The green power schemes were also differentiated in the market place by offering slightly different packages, although there are two basic types, supply and fund schemes. Supply schemes promise to match the power consumers use with power bought in from renewable sources.

In some of these green power supply schemes, a surcharge is usually made, levied to meet the extra cost – 10–15 per cent extra depending on the scheme. However, in recognition of the argument that energy efficiency and renewables are compatible, some of the green power schemes included energy efficiency packages to offset the extra cost of the green power. For example, offering consumers free compact fluorescent lamps or advice on cutting energy use.

Fund schemes, rather than offsetting consumers' electricity with green power, like the supply schemes, offer consumers an opportunity to pay into a fund to support the development of renewable energy projects. Other electricity companies offer a hybrid between supply and fund schemes.

By 2003 around 60 000 UK consumers had signed up to a green power scheme of some sort, rising to around 150 000 by early 2005. In the supply schemes, participating consumers are usually able to identify the sources used, for example a wind farm. This may not be your own technology, and it may not be a local plant, but it does make some sort of link between what you get out of the socket in the wall and the source of the power. Moreover, in fund schemes, consumers usually donate a surcharge direct to a trust that invests in specific renewable energy projects, usually locally. So, in that case, there is an even more direct sense of local involvement.

Most green power consumers in the UK are enthusiastic, whether they have signed up to supply schemes or to fund schemes. One supply scheme customer commented, 'I just like the idea of the electricity for the home coming from a renewable source. Of course I know it's not actually renewable electricity as such, but the equivalent amount of electricity is being pumped into the grid as a result of what we draw from it.'

However, others were keen on the fund schemes, like EcoPower, which was set up by what was then Eastern Energy in 1998, through which consumers pay extra to a fund for local renewable projects. One consumer said,

> We decided to go for EcoPower because we wanted to support green electricity and EcoPower seemed a good scheme in that the money is being used to support small-scale community projects that are bringing a direct benefit to the Eastern Region. To begin with I was sceptical but actually having thought about it I like the fact that it's encouraging Eastern Energy to do what they can to increase renewable energy supplies and supplying small scale local solutions to energy issues rather than these large-scale infrastructure projects that cause their own problems.

(NATTA, 2002)

3.4 Impact on technology diffusion

The green power schemes may have been effective at consciousness raising about environmental issues and the potential role of renewables, and that can play a role in easing the diffusion of these technologies. But how effective have the schemes been in directly stimulating the development and deployment of the technology? In particular, what was the impact of consumer involvement?

Most of the fund schemes issue annual brochures describing the projects that have been supported with the extra money paid by consumers, and inviting feedback. Many of the funds are actually run as independent trusts, often with a representative of an environmental organisation invited to sit on the management committee. These committees are usually keen to hear what consumers say about prospective and actual projects.

The scale of the funds has so far been relatively small. In the first year of their operation (2000–01) the fund schemes attracted only around £150 000 from consumers, although in some cases the supply companies matched this with their own funds. This initial funding nevertheless led to nine new renewable energy projects around the UK, mostly small local community projects, involving wind, photovoltaic solar (PV), or micro hydro. They included a 3-kilowatt micro hydro project in Staffordshire, supported by npower under its Evergreen scheme. An 800-watt PV project at the Greenhouse in Norwich was supported by Eastern Energy's EcoPower scheme. EcoPower also backed a small wind turbine at a winery. Scottish Power supported three community projects.

At the launch of the hydro scheme in Staffordshire in 2001, npower's spokesperson commented,

> We think it's quite important that people, particularly on a community basis, see practical applications of power and power generation, because it can be altogether big frightening technology, way back in some engineer's scheming mind. What we've got here is a practical demonstration where people can come and say ah yes, I can see how it works. I understand what renewable means now. And so we think there's a big customer awareness and educational process as a result of doing these things in a local community.

With the supply schemes there are usually fewer opportunities for interaction with consumers. However, the supply companies do sometimes indicate that specific investments in renewable energy projects have been the result of demand for the green power from consumers collectively. Both Northern Ireland Electricity and Scottish Power have indicated that their support for new wind farms was a consequence of growing demand from consumers.

In addition to schemes run by the large conventional energy retail companies – for instance the various regional electricity companies, Powergen and npower – there have also been notable interventions by smaller independent companies. Indeed, one based in the Stroud area, and initially called the Renewable Energy Company, was a pioneer in the field, supplying local consumers direct from green power bought locally. Subsequently, under the name Ecotricity, it became a major player in the renewable energy field, supporting the development of some large projects, such as the 1.3-megawatt-rated wind turbine at Swaffham in Norfolk and a 4.8-megawatt-rated wind farm with eight turbines in Lincolnshire (see Box 3 for an explanation of power units). By September 2004 the Ecotricity green tariff scheme had over 5000 subscribers, including some large companies. By late 2005 it had 12 000 domestic subscribers.

Box 3   Energy and power units

Energy

People, including technologists, talk about energy consumption, and that term is used in this course. It would be more accurate to talk about energy conversion. When you climb a flight of stairs, you are converting the energy from the food you consumed into the energy your muscles need. The faster you climb, or the more you carry at the same speed, the more power you develop – in other words, the faster you convert energy.

The joule is the SI unit of energy. However the kilowatt-hour (kWh) is the energy unit used for energy generation and consumption – it is the standard unit by which electricity is sold.

1 kWh is the energy generated or consumed when a 1-kW-rated device runs for one hour. A megawatt-hour is 1000 kilowatt-hours.

It is helpful to know how much the average woman, man or child consumes in one 24-hour period. Using figures for world energy consumption and world population, a person consumes over 50 kWh of energy per day (Boyle et al, 2003).

Power

The watt is the SI unit of power. Roughly, a human being can develop 125 watts of continuous power (Elert, 2003), which comes from joules (calories) being converted as a result of muscle action.

A kilowatt (kW) is 1000 watts, and 1 megawatt (MW) is 1000 kilowatts.

Which unit?

The literature about energy and power can be confusing because units for energy consumption (kilowatt-hour) and power (watt) often occur together. It is usual to give the maximum achievable energy conversion (power) of a machine in watts, for example a large nuclear or coal-fired power station will typically be capable of generating 1000 megawatts of electricity. Whereas a power station's average daily output will be measured in megawatt-hours – on a particular day it may produce no more than half of what it is capable.

Another pioneering independent company, initially trading as UnitE, also offered green power from local sources, and under the name Good Energy was subsequently acclaimed by some environmentalists, including Friends of the Earth, as the greenest of the green power supply schemes. That was because it was seen as the 'only available one which ensures that you receive electricity from renewable energy above that which suppliers need to obtain to meet their legal obligations' (Green Electricity, undated).

However, in order to do this, Good Energy has to charge significantly more than the normal price for electricity. Even so, by mid 2005 it had around 16 000 subscribers. By contrast, npower sought consumer involvement, or at least endorsement, with its 'zero premium' green power supply scheme, Juice, which was launched in 2001 in conjunction with Greenpeace. The aim was to use power from its offshore wind farm at North Hoyle, 7 km off the North Wales coast, at that time still under development. This project opened in 2003, but in the interim, Juice supplies came from existing onshore wind sources and a small hydro plant in Snowdonia. By the end of 2004, with the offshore wind farm fully operational, over 40 000 consumers had signed up.

Despite being linked to a major renewable energy project, as a zero premium scheme with no surcharge, consumers signing up to Juice are not investing extra in the new wind project, other than by paying the normal amount for their electricity to npower. But the scheme was seen as providing a way for consumers to show support for renewables. More practically, the scheme also included a fund element, via a commitment by npower to allocate £10 annually per Juice customer, up to a limit of £500 000 total annually, to support renewable projects. Matthew Thomas, Juice project leader for npower, said,

> We believe Juice will help kick-start the renewable energy revolution in the UK. Consumers can now invest in the future of clean energy, and show their support for wind power, without paying more.

In 2005, following up their commitment to supporting other areas of development, npower allocated £195 000 from the Juice fund to the regional agency Regen SW to help them develop their wave energy programme. npower said this was the first of many awards from the fund, which would support a range of newly emerging renewables, such as wave, tidal and solar.

 The T307 DVD includes a video on UK green power retail schemes and consumer responses to them (see the *Block 4 Guide*).

3.5   Future of green power schemes

The UK is not alone in having green power retail schemes. Most industrialised countries now have some form of green power retailing. The scale of consumer take-up of these various offerings has varied around the world.

Some of the first schemes were in Australia and the USA. The first green tariff scheme in Australia was launched in 1998, with 28 500 domestic consumers signing up, rising to over 87 000 by 2003. In the USA there was initially a lot of enthusiasm for the idea of what are called green tariff schemes, with initially over 100 000 consumers signing up in California after the launch of the first scheme there in 1998.

However, the Californian energy market crisis in 2000–01, which led to erratic energy price swings and the collapse of some energy supply companies, in effect killed off most of the schemes there, although progress continues to be made in other states. By 2003 around 500 000 people across the USA had their electricity supplied under a green tariff scheme of some type, and the growing level of interest from consumers led companies to invest in more capacity to meet demand.

According to researchers from the US National Renewable Energy Laboratory, by 2004 about 1400 megawatts of new renewable energy generating capacity was supported in part through consumer demand for green energy – roughly equivalent to one nuclear power plant. This was despite green power costing more. A review of the top 10 US utility schemes in 2004 found the premiums they charged were in the range 1.3–0.59 cent/kilowatt-hour (see Box 3 for an explanation of energy units). In those 10 utility schemes the power from wind was offered in eight of them, solar in one, geothermal in one, landfill gas in four, and hydro in two.

In continental Europe diffusion was initially slower, but it grew quite rapidly. For example, by 2002 around 280 000 consumers had signed up in Germany and around 1.2 million in the Netherlands. By 2003 the EU total had reached nearly 2.5 million consumers and by 2004 over 3 million. Initially, consumers who signed up to green power schemes in the Netherlands could benefit from a reduction to the energy tax that had been imposed, but this incentive was gradually removed. In most other countries consumers have had to pay significantly more for green power right from the start, but clearly they have not been put off by the higher prices. As noted at the start of this section in relation to energy prices in the UK, consumers are not always motivated just by economics. The pattern of support is influenced by price, but perhaps not always as might be expected.

Case study   Willing-to-pay analysis

Although the price of electricity will be an important factor shaping consumer responses and choices, these responses will also reflect a range of attitudes to other issues, including attitudes to the environment. One technique used by researchers in this field – and in environmental economics and marketing generally – is to ask what price consumers are willing to pay for a green scheme or product to build up a quantitative picture of their attitudes and sensitivities. The results of a willing-to-pay analysis in relation to green power schemes in Germany are shown in Figure 9. The figure shows the levels of willingness to pay at various percentage price increase levels, for a range of age groups.

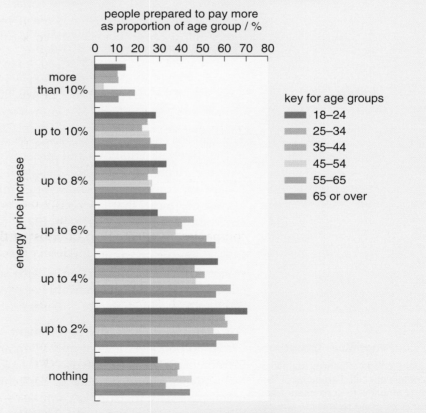

Figure 9   Many German consumers are willing to pay extra for green energy Source: data from Datamonitor Europe, 2002

As the figure shows, and as you would expect, the numbers willing to pay fall off with increasing price. But even so, depending on the age group, 23–34 per cent of those asked said they would be willing to pay up to 10 per cent more. Notice there are some interesting variations among the different age groups at the various levels of price. The young and the old seem more willing to pay more than the middle aged, at most, but not all, levels.

Of course there may be a significant difference between what people say they might be willing to do and what they actually do. For example, there were some optimistic initial reports of likely consumer responses to green power schemes in the UK that have not translated into reality. For example, 65 per cent of those asked in a MORI opinion poll survey in 1996 said they would prefer to buy green power, although only if it did not cost more, while 21 per cent said they would be prepared to pay more for it. In the event, as noted earlier, by 2003 only about 0.3 per cent of UK households had signed up – this may have been due to lack of consumer awareness. When zero premium schemes like Juice started to advertise more forcefully, the total rose so that by the end of 2004 the total was around 150 000, with Juice having 40 000 of these subscribers.

Even so, there were much higher take-up figures in countries like the Netherlands and Germany, where the government and the energy supply companies both pushed green power retail schemes strongly. A rule of thumb in such situations is that around 10–15 per cent of those who say they might be willing to buy into such schemes actually do so. However, the rate of the adoption in the Netherlands seems to have been higher than is implied by this rule – by 2003 there were 2.2 million subscribers to green power schemes, representing nearly 33 per cent of the country's households. Part of the explanation for this is that initially consumers could avail themselves of a reduction in their energy tax when they signed up to a green power scheme. Although this incentive was gradually phased out, and was removed entirely by 2005, consumers in the Netherlands seem likely to continue to sign up to green power schemes, albeit at a lower rate. A survey in 2002 found that 46 per cent said they were willing to pay up to 15 per cent more for green energy. By 2004, 2.8 million households had signed up, over 40 per cent of the total households in the country.

The reasons for the different levels of diffusion in different countries lie in the different situations and structures found in each country. The way the green power market has been structured in the UK has made it hard for consumers to show much enthusiasm and does not necessarily mean that UK consumers are economically conservative or environmentally insensitive. Section 7 of this block will describe in more detail how, rather than stimulating demand for green power from domestic consumers, the UK government has increasingly preferred to focus support on what it sees as more direct ways of stimulating the use of renewable energy technologies, with mechanisms aimed chiefly at energy suppliers.

Renewables Obligation

requirement on electricity suppliers to obtain specified amounts of the energy they sell to consumers from generators using renewable energy

For example, in 2002, the government imposed a Renewables Obligation on electricity supply companies requiring them to incrementally increase the use of renewables so that by 2010 these technologies would provide 10 per cent of all the electricity sold. The green electricity the supply companies buy under this scheme is simply mixed in with the rest, and sold to consumers as usual. However, the energy suppliers are allowed to pass on any extra costs to consumers via their normal electricity bills. Consumers have no influence over this process, they all pay, whether or not they are signed up to green power schemes.

Crucially, the rules of the Renewables Obligation do not allow supply companies to use any of the electricity bought to meet the obligation in supplying domestic green power schemes, for which extra is normally charged. Otherwise consumers could in effect be paying two surcharges. Power for green power tariff supply schemes has to come from sources that are additional to those being used to meet the obligation, and there are not many of them. That is why supply schemes like Good Energy have to charge significant premiums – they have to operate using power outside the Renewables Obligation system, though this may be generated by the same sources as those that meet their obligation quota.

The result of this rule has been that in the UK, what is sometimes called the voluntary green market, has not expanded as much as might be expected. Most energy supply companies have not promoted the schemes strongly, in part because they did not have access to sufficient additional green power to sell, and most of the available renewable power has instead gone to meet demand created by support mechanisms such as the Renewables Obligation.

Some people argue that it is more equitable and effective for all consumers to contribute to developing renewables, through the Renewables Obligation, rather than leaving it to a few altruistic individuals as with the voluntary green power schemes. By contrast, there are clearly consumers who want to make a personal commitment, and the voluntary schemes provide a way. Certainly that is the message from the rest of Europe. For example, given that domestic electricity accounts for about 30 per cent of total electricity use, the voluntary green power market accounted for around 10 per cent of the total electricity demand in the Netherlands. This should be compared with the UK's target of obtaining 10 per cent of its electricity from renewables by 2010, using mainstream mechanisms like the Renewables Obligation.

climate change levy
a tax imposed on the energy used by most UK companies, unless they make use of renewable sources

Clearly the UK has adopted a different approach, leaving the voluntary domestic market to survive on the margins. By contrast, in the business sector in the UK, things are somewhat different. The climate change levy, which was introduced in 2001, is creating substantial demand for green power, because most businesses, but not domestic consumers, are charged 0.43 pence/kilowatt extra for electricity, unless it is obtained from renewable sources. As a result, companies signed up direct to electricity suppliers for green power. In 2002, the first year of operation, around 6 800 000 megawatt-hours of energy was contracted for company use. That is nearly all the green power that was produced in that year, around 2 per cent of the UK's total electricity generation.

As well as industry and commerce, subscribers include many local authorities, universities, and community organisations. Some of these organisations may have a direct interest in the development of renewables; for example, the Body Shop and Co-operative Bank have both been subscribing to a green power scheme for some while, and offer their customers access to a voluntary green power scheme run by Ecotricity, one of the green power pioneers.

3.6 Conclusion

This section has looked at the extent of consumer take-up of energy efficiency measures and green power retail schemes and at the role these consumer options can play in reducing climate-changing greenhouse gas emissions from the domestic sector.

Although take-up of green energy is relatively low, it is expected that this will increase as renewable energy reduces in cost and fossil fuels become more expensive. Energy conservation is, however, already attractive in that, over time, it can save money, although, as you have seen, there are also problems that can limit its uptake and its impact.

From a sustainability point of view green power schemes need to be coupled with energy conservation to try to deal with the problem of increasing energy consumption in the domestic sector. The efficient use of energy and the use of green power services for the energy can work together offering consumers the option of reducing their environmental impacts without too much extra expense. Increasing consumer demand for green power schemes can also help stimulate demand for new renewable energy projects.

SAQ 2

What factors might limit the rate of take up of green power tariff schemes by UK domestic consumers?

Key points of Section 3

- There is a range of green products and services on offer to consumers, including electricity supply services and energy conservation aids.

- Some consumers say they are willing to pay more to energy supply companies to support the use of renewable energy sources, but fewer actually do, although this varies from country to country.

- The green power retail market provides a way for consumers to create demand for green power, thereby stimulating energy supply companies to support the use and development of renewable energy technologies.

- Many consumers have signed up to green power schemes in the EU generally, but the level of take-up is less in the UK, possibly due to the different support arrangements for green power – supply companies cannot contract to sell power claimed against the Renewables Obligation to the voluntary green power market.

- By contrast the take-up of energy efficiency measures is larger, but the resultant energy savings may be undermined by the continued rise in demand for energy and by the rebound effect.

- Switching over to using cleaner fossil fuels like gas in power stations can help reduce emissions but using renewable energy sources can eliminate them.

- However, because renewables currently cost more, a combined renewables-plus-efficiency approach, with energy saving measures in effect subsidising the use of renewable energy, could be beneficial.

The key points for Section 3 meet learning outcome 1.4.

4 Empowered consumers

4.1 Specialist consumers

In this section you will look at how consumers have been involved with renewable energy technologies in a more radical and proactive way. In the previous section you saw how consumers could support the development of renewable energy through subscribing to green power schemes. This section looks at consumers who have gone a step further to install and use new energy technologies themselves. This is clearly a much more proactive approach requiring a significant commitment on the part of the consumer.

In the early days of renewable energy technologies this approach was adopted by small groups of enthusiasts. However, problems with existing energy systems and power supplies in some countries do seem to be leading to more widespread adoption of new approaches. As you read earlier, in the USA some consumers are buying renewable energy technologies for their homes because existing power services are unreliable as well as environmentally worrying. Similar developments could occur in the UK as concern about environmental issues grows and with the availability of new types of micropower devices.

Such developments are the topic of this section, which seeks to explore the way in which consumers and users with special interests or concerns support the development and marketing of new products. At present, there are relatively few specialist consumers using renewable energy technologies. A review in 2006 estimated that fewer than 100 000 domestic-scale micropower units had been installed in the UK – mostly roof-mounted water systems heated by the sun. Growth in numbers in the future could stimulate investment in new renewable energy projects and new technologies. If self-generation becomes widespread, consumers could influence corporate technological development radically through their novel purchasing decisions.

4.2 California power crisis

In 2000–01 there was a crisis with the power system in California, with regular blackouts and sudden large price increases. The main cause of the crisis was the deregulation of the energy market. Market liberalisation, or deregulation as it is called in the USA, was seen as a way to increase competition and reduce prices, but the effect in California was disastrous.

There seem to be as many explanations of exactly what happened, and why it happened, as there are analysts. However, it seems the key to the crisis was that as part of the deregulation exercises, a fixed consumer energy price ceiling was imposed. This measure was reasonable enough but when there was an upsurge in demand, wholesale prices shot up. This led to the collapse of some of the key power retail companies who could not (initially) pass the extra cost to consumers and could not operate with the lower profit margins that resulted.

The crisis was institutional and regulatory rather than technological, although there was a technological element. Economic pressures in the electricity market, coupled with environmental controls on plant construction, had meant there had been less investment in new capacity and in grid maintenance and development. The result was that when electricity demand began to rise – particularly because of the increasing use of computers and air conditioners – the system could not cope. Importing power from outside California was both difficult and expensive. It has also been argued that some of the supply companies were faced with what are rather quaintly called 'stranded assets' in the form of nuclear power plants, which could not compete in the new more competitive market, but had to be kept going and paid for to maintain supplies.

There were claims that some of the power shortages were contrived, and that some of the companies involved had manipulated the market, withholding power to boost profits. This appears to have been confirmed when in October 2002 the former chief trader of Enron's West Power Trading Division in Portland, Oregon, agreed to plead guilty to a charge of conspiracy.

Whatever the full explanation of the cause, the result was clear. With demand exceeding supply, wholesale prices had shot up dramatically. During some periods in 2001 some supply companies were being charged up to 50 times more than normal for short-term, peak-demand electricity, leading some of them to go bust. Consumer prices shot through the imposed ceiling. But that was not enough and a rotating, area-by-area, blackout programme had to be imposed.

With regular power blackouts and electricity bills hiked by 40 per cent or more, some consumers in California turned to using photovoltaic solar (PV) systems, installing solar cell modules on their rooftops, even though it was still an expensive way to generate electricity (Figure 10). To some extent it was a protest action. One consumer told the local *Orange County Register*, 'I'm outraged that large corporate powers can band together and apparently charge whatever they want for power. We're all hostage now to a consortium of electric-power suppliers.' And the owner of Solar Electrical Systems in Thousand Oaks said, 'People have started saying they've had enough. They want some control in their lives, and don't want to be a pawn of Southern California Edison and the state.'

However, it was not just a protest response. It also began to look like a realistic energy option, with demand for the technology beginning to grow. The California Energy Commission, which offers 50 per cent rebates on the cost of installing PV systems, took 450 applications from solar buyers in the first two months of 2001, nearly the same amount as received in the three previous years combined. It saw interest in solar systems rise by 500 per cent in the first two years after the energy crisis.

The expansion in consumer interest was clearly helped by support not only from state-wide programmes like this, but also from programmes run by local public agencies. For example, the Los Angeles Department of Water and Power (LADWP) introduced a quite generous solar rooftop incentive program, which subsidised the purchase and installation of grid-connected PV for a customer's home or business. The incentive amounted to $3 per watt of generating capacity for systems manufactured outside the city, $5 per watt for systems

Figure 10   Photovoltaic solar installation in the USA Source: US Department of Energy. Photovoltaic modules are made up of solar cells that convert sunlight directly into electricity. The conversion efficiency is low but the technology is developing rapidly and costs continue to fall.

manufactured inside the LA city boundary. LADWP offered to pay up to $50 000 for each residential system, and up to $1 million for a commercial installation.

There were, however, some conditions. The household systems could supply, on average, no more than 100 per cent of the customer's own power needs. Customers had net metering – a meter that runs backwards – so they could offset the cost of the power they bought from the suppliers with the power they generated themselves, but they were not allowed to actually make a profit by selling power, over and above what they consumed. Moreover, the incentive did not cover the purchase of energy storage systems, which could only be connected to the grid. From LADWP's point of view, the company got more solar generating capacity installed, using consumers' rooftops, part funded by the consumer, and they could resell any excess solar electricity to other customers on the grid. Consumers who were not happy with these restrictions and who wanted to be able to generate excess power for others to buy would not get the installation subsidy and would, in effect, have to become independent power producers.

Similar constraints were imposed on some of the other schemes that emerged in California, for example the self-generation incentive program (SGIP) run by Southern California Edison. This programme provided financial incentives to customers to install certain kinds and sizes of 'clean' on-site distributed generation – up to 1.5 megawatts. However, it only applied to facilities that operated in parallel with the electricity grid, which means such systems could not be used for stand-alone back-up generation. Nevertheless, by 2004 over 100 megawatts of new capacity had been supported.

This scheme was actually designed primarily with business and large institutional customers in mind. A parallel California Energy Commission scheme was more specifically geared to smaller domestic self-generation of less than 30-kilowatt capacity. By mid 2001 this had led to around 2500 applications and the installation of around 14 megawatts of capacity, much of it PV solar. By 2004, around 7500 projects had been supported under this scheme and overall, between 2001 and 2004, more than 11 000 PV systems were installed in California. Similar developments have emerged in New England and elsewhere in the USA, particularly after the blackout across much of the US North East in 2003.

Like many other grass-roots groups, the long-running US Institute for Local Self-Reliance had been promoting the idea of renewable energy technologies for many years, but it is the problem with the grid supply that has finally led to increasing diffusion. The institute's director, David Morris, in his book *Seeing the Light: Regaining Control of our Electricity System* says,

> Policy makers and customers are looking to regain control over their electricity system, bringing power, both literally and figuratively, to the people.

He argues that citizens must 'take charge of their electrons' if they hope to regain reliability and peace of mind:

> American citizens must reject regulated power utilities and deregulation, and take control of their own distribution and transmission grids.

(Morris, 2001)

Morris outlines the steps that are necessary to develop a flexible network of small-scale power plants including rooftop PV solar. He says that consumers and communities have started to move in this direction, and the energy crisis in California has encouraged them to 'redefine their electric futures in ways that achieve reliability and low cost, as well as social and environmental goals'. Clearly the blackouts helped win support. One consumer who had already converted to PV crystallised the point neatly by saying 'Blackout? What blackout?'

4.3 Domestic-level self-generation in the UK

Self-generation has a long history in rural areas in the USA, and may now be of interest to urban consumers. But what about the UK? Until recently, interest in self-generation has mainly been limited to a few people in remote off-grid areas. But in the 1980s and 1990s interest grew in rooftop solar water heating systems. Subsequently some enthusiasts also took up the more expensive solar PV option for electricity generation.

The UK government had not seen solar PV as relevant for use in the UK, and had not provided much support, but some pioneers pushed on, using what support was available. The first major UK project was a private house in north Oxford, owned by Susan Roaf, a professor at the Oxford School of Architecture. The house was completed in 1995, with a grant from the government. Its 4-kilowatt-rated integral PV roof provides most of the power needed over a typical year, although there is also a small roof-mounted solar collector for water heating and a biomass stove to provide back-up heating (Figure 11). During the summer the PV array produces excess power, which is sold to the grid, but during the winter Roaf occasionally needs to top up by importing power from the grid.

Figure 11 Susan Roaf's PV roof on her house in Oxford As well as producing most of the electricity needed over the year, some of the power produced is used to charge batteries in a small electric vehicle

An ex-Greenpeace energy campaigner subsequently set up a company, Solar Century, which successfully promoted solar PV systems to a wide range of consumers. Figure 12 shows one of the first of their projects, a terraced house in south London with the conventional roof slates replaced with solar tiles.

Figure 12 Solar tiles being laid on a house roof in the UK
Source: Solarcentury

With Germany, the USA and Japan all pushing ahead with major PV deployment programmes, the UK government changed its view and in 2002 launched a £20m PV demonstration programme, with the aim of supporting the installation of PV systems on 3000 domestic roofs and 140 larger non-residential buildings. It offered grants for 50 per cent of the cost. By 2004 the programme had supported over 400 projects, with a total of over 5000 kilowatts of generating capacity,

In the same year, the Energy Minister, Mike O'Brien, announced an extra £8.5m in grant funding for small-scale renewables projects, including PV solar, for schools, houses and commercial buildings. O'Brien said,

In future, energy generation will often be small scale and local. We need to change the way we think about energy. That starts at grass-roots level, in our homes and communities. ... Initiatives such as these help to deliver the message that as well as being responsible for energy consumption we can play a part in producing it as well.

You will be looking at grass-roots orientated government support schemes of this type, including the £10 million Clear Skies community energy programme, in Section 10.

However, even with the government support programme, individual domestic consumers may still find it hard to afford the significant capital cost of installing their own energy generation equipment, especially PV solar.

This problem can be partly offset by the development of electricity tariff schemes that allow consumers to earn reasonable payback rates for any excess electricity they sell back to the grid. Susan Roaf only received around 2 pence/kilowatt-hour for any excess power she offered from her Oxford PV solar house to her local electricity company, but had to pay the full conventional price of around 6 pence/kilowatt-hour for any electricity she bought from them. However, under the newly emerging net metering schemes, there is just one standard charge for the net amount of power transferred. In effect the consumer's meter goes backwards when they are supplying power to the grid, so the supply company may end up owing consumers money, and the PV roof begins to pay back its cost more rapidly.

In addition to net metering arrangements, some schemes emerged to provide more financial support, augmenting the government PV support programme. For example, the Going Solar scheme, launched in 2003, brought together the Royal Society for the Protection of Birds, the promoter of the scheme, with PV supplier Solar Century, the Energy Saving Trust (EST), the Co-operative Bank and Scottish and Southern Electricity (SSE), to provide a package of funding for photovoltaics as well as solar water heating. The EST helps consumers to obtain grants from the Department of Trade and Industry, and the remainder of the capital cost can be borrowed on a low-rate loan from the Co-operative Bank. SSE then buys any excess electricity produced by customers via a net metering arrangement.

PV solar is obviously only one example of a technology that could be used for self-generation at the domestic house level. Some householders have also adopted solar heat collection to provide space heating and water heating, this being a much less expensive option than PV.

The following case study looks at some other options for both heat and electricity, including various micro-combined heat and power (micro-CHP) units, and, in the longer term, fuel cells. As can be seen, these new technologies offer the possibility that domestic consumers could generate most if not all their energy themselves, although with these technologies, unlike solar technologies, the fuel (gas) still has to be bought in.

Case study | Technology for self-generation

Self-generation by consumers, as opposed to using power delivered by the national electricity grid from centralised power plants, may initially seem an unlikely development, but so at one time did the idea that centralised mainframe computers could be replaced by personal computers. Interest in domestic-level energy generation has focused not just on renewables like solar heating or PV solar, but also on other types of small-scale energy generation technologies which use fossil fuels more efficiently, including the well-established heat pump technology. This is essentially a refrigerator working in reverse, which uses electricity to pump heat from the ground, or some other low temperature heat source, into a building to provide space heating, with high levels of efficiency.

In addition, some novel small-scale electricity plants have begun to emerge. For example, in 2003 the British Gas subsidiary Microgen introduced a revolutionary superefficient, domestic combined heat and micro-CHP power plant that produces electricity as well as heat, using a Stirling engine running on natural gas. The Stirling engine concept was first developed a century ago and various designs have emerged over the years. Stirling engines work by using an external heat source to expand a working fluid, often helium, contained in a piston cylinder. They can be efficient and quiet, running with little need for maintenance, which makes them attractive for domestic use. They also look unexceptional, just like a conventional gas boiler unit (Figure 13).

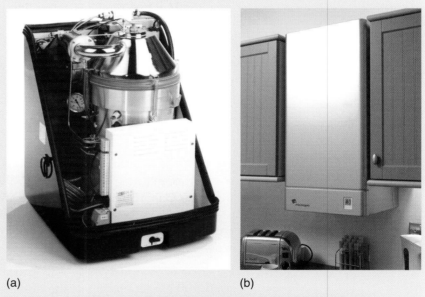

(a)   (b)

Figure 13   (a) WhisperGen domestic micro-CHP unit. (b) British Gas-Microgen domestic CHP unit. Sources: (a) Onboard Energy; (b) Microgen

The new Microgen unit was expected to cost around £2000, about £600 to £700 more than a conventional condensing gas boiler. However, expected savings on the average domestic electricity bill were about £150 a year, meaning the extra cost of the boiler could be recouped in five years. The expectation is that, within a decade, there could be one million in use.

In parallel, Powergen introduced its micro-CHP Stirling engine unit, based on WhisperGen technology it had developed jointly with New Zealand company Whisper Tech. In 2004 a version capable of 8 kilowatts of heat and up to 2 kilowatts of electricity was produced. It was expected to cost £3000 to buy and install. PowerGen estimates that by 2020 at least 30 per cent of UK households will use a micro-CHP system and that over half of all UK homes will be suitable for installation, most likely on a gradual basis, when boilers need replacing or in new-build homes.

With both the BG Microgen system and the Powergen system, the consumer remains linked to the electricity grid, which still provides the bulk of their electric power, but they can sell back any excess power they generate to their electricity supplier. The longer-term vision is therefore that houses could become power stations, supplying some power to the grid.

As can be seen, it is possible that self-generation, whether using renewable energy systems like solar PV, or natural gas fired micro-plants, could become widespread. Longer term there are also even more advanced technological options, including the use of fuel cells, devices that convert hydrogen gas into electricity, operating something like electrolysis in reverse. They can be run on natural gas from the gas main or even from biogas produced from local sources, although most fuel cells require the methane gas to be chemically converted to hydrogen.

Ultimately, as natural gas becomes scarce and expensive, and to reduce the greenhouse gas emissions produced by using it as fuel, it may be that there will be a shift to using pure hydrogen as a new fuel. It can be generated by the electrolysis of water using electricity from renewable sources, and it could be delivered to consumers by pipe, as with the gas main. When and if a shift to what has been called the 'hydrogen economy' happens, then self-generation of electricity by consumers when they need it may even replace delivery of electricity by the national grid.

For the moment, however, this is still a long way off, although there are already some interesting experimental projects using hydrogen for independent stand-alone energy supply. For example, in 2004 West Beacon farm in Leicestershire installed a 34-kilowatt electrolyser to convert excess power from its existing wind, solar and hydro generators to hydrogen. This gas is then stored and converted back to electricity when needed in a fuel cell. The fuel cell also generates some heat, which is collected and used, so the complete system is operated as a CHP plant.

Independent generation, using advanced technologies like this, may still be only experimental, and totally autonomous systems, running independently of the grid, are not necessarily what will be needed in countries like the UK, except perhaps in isolated off-grid areas. While the use of independent solar may spread, for most people in the industrialised countries interested in self-generation, domestic micro-CHP is likely to be the most obvious option. These systems still of course need gas to be supplied from the grid, and some feed excess power back to the grid, but they do generate power locally.

In 2004 just over 7 per cent of the world's electricity was generated independently, including by businesses and industrial users who are increasingly finding it attractive to generate power themselves. The World Alliance for Decentralized Energy set a global target of increasing this to 14 per cent by 2012 (WADE, 2005). However, in some remote areas in developing countries, fully independent off-grid generation may be the only option – around 2 billion people in the world have no access to gas or electricity grids and little hope of grid power being provided.

The following case study looks at another novel idea, a micro-wind turbine for domestic use, which could be used as an alternative or additional to the use of solar devices.

Case study | Micro-wind turbines

In 2003, Scottish inventor David Gordon launched a small 750-watt-rated wind power system, Windsave, designed to be fitted on almost any roof or wall to supplement electricity from the grid; the power feeds directly into the domestic supply via a mains plug. Gordon claimed that it could provide up to 15 per cent of the annual electricity needs of an average house, depending on location. In 2004, a version was put on sale for an installation cost of around £1000 plus VAT. By mid 2005 the company reported that 10 000 orders had been received and a contract had been made with gas supplier Centrica, which it was claimed could lead to sales of up to 100 000 units, because of Centrica's large customer base (16 million).

In addition to cutting their fuel bills directly, consumers can also earn money from the power produced because the Windsave system includes remote metering technology, which allows each unit to be automatically phoned every quarter to see how much electricity it has generated. The company will then collect credits for this power via the government's Renewables Obligation scheme (discussed in Section 3). The resulting Renewables Obligation certificates are traded by Windsave to provide some payback to the consumers involved. (You will look at certificate trading schemes like this in more detail in Section 9.)

The idea of using the Renewables Obligation system in this way is clearly something of an innovation. The consumers become, in effect, part of a distributed energy self-generation network, which allows them to get an extra financial benefit from the energy they produce. On this basis, and assuming that consumers could also get a grant for installation under the government's Clear Skies scheme, the payback period (the time taken to pay back the consumers' capital outlay from energy saved and from Renewables Obligation certificates) could be 5–6 years, depending on location.

The Windsave machine is not the only small wind turbine on the market. For example, for many years Marlec has produced popular micro-wind units, widely used for battery charging for yachts, caravans and the like. The Scottish company Proven has also sold several hundred of its mini turbines for domestic use. Throughout the 2000s, in addition to the Windsave, a range of other small wind rotors designed specifically for rooftops emerged around the world, like the Swift (Figure 14).

Figure 14 Renewable Devices' 1.5 kilowatt Swift rooftop micro-wind turbine The ring connecting the blades is claimed to increase efficiency and reduce blade noise

The Swift was developed by a group of researchers in a small Scottish technology development company called Renewable Devices. Some early versions were installed on local schools, and then, following a £9.2m manufacturing and supply agreement with Scottish and Southern Energy plc, volume production began in 2005, with the aim being to get the cost of installing the device down to around £1500. The developers said they expected the payback time would be around three years, depending on location, and claimed the system would have an operational lifetime of 20 years. Like the Windsave, it plugs directly into the mains.

If the idea catches on, small turbines might be sited on tops of many buildings, especially high-rise buildings where wind speeds can be high. Hammersmith Council in London experimented with one on the roof of a 22-storey residential block, and others are likely to follow. Small wind turbines are nowhere near as efficient as larger devices because the power available from wind turbines is proportional to the square of the blade diameter, and larger machines are usually sited in windy areas.

Small wind devices should not need planning permission, especially if sited below the highest point of houses, although, as with satellite dishes, there can sometimes be planning challenges, for example in conservation areas. Clearly, care must be taken with siting to avoid any safety risk from the moving blades; some designs have the rotor contained in shrouds or integrated into the building structure. But because they can produce power where it is needed, without the need for long, expensive and energy-inefficient transmission links, wind turbines may begin to be used in urban environments as well as the more familiar rural locations.

Certainly, at the time of writing, domestic micro-wind units are far cheaper per kilowatt installed and per kilowatt-hour of delivered energy than PV solar systems, although micro-wind is still something of a novelty. Nevertheless, the idea of installing micro-wind, possibly as well as PV systems, seems to be catching on, aided by support from companies like Good Energy, the green energy retailer. In May 2004, it launched a home generation scheme, designed to help promote the use of micro-renewable power by paying small renewable generators 4 pence/kWh for the power generated by their renewable installations, with part of this payment reflecting the value of the Renewables Obligation credits, which Good Energy claims on the consumer's behalf. By the end of 2004, Good Energy had 87 home generator customers, 20 per cent of which were micro-wind and 80 per cent of which were solar photovoltaics, and it expected to have a total of 400 home generators by the end of 2005.

Who will adopt new technologies like this? Clearly they are likely to be what Rogers called innovators and early adopters. An interesting insight into their motivations comes from research carried out in conjunction with a field test of domestic micro-CHP fuel cell units in Germany in 2003. The focus was on the innovators, called pioneers by the research team. The researchers noted that the role of pioneers was 'to test and help develop the new technology and to propagate it, paving its way into a broader market' (Fischer, 2005).

For the moment engagement with new developments like this may only interest pioneers. But such engagement is an important part of the overall innovation process, for as indicated by many of the case studies in this block, that is how innovations both develop and spread.

Case study | Micro-CHP in Germany

Pioneer households for testing micro-CHP fuel cell units were sought out by means of advertisements in regional newspapers. Although only 25 prototypes were planned to be tested, over 6000 households volunteered. After a review of the suitability of the buildings, about 1000 volunteers remained. The arrangement was that the volunteer households would receive a home heating system that functioned as a combined heat and power plant, generating electricity that could be used in the household or fed into the grid.

It was a contracting arrangement because the system remained the property of the utility company that was responsible for maintenance and operation. Users paid average tariffs for heat and electricity from the plant. Furthermore, they had to pay a one-time innovation contribution of 2000 euro. If the plant failed, the power utility had to replace it or provide a substitute, so the user's supply was guaranteed. Users in turn had to provide access to engineers and technicians for monitoring purposes. So, not only there was no financial incentive involved, but also there was also some inconvenience for the users, and it was by no means clear the new technology would work reliably and satisfactorily.

Corinna Fischer (2004) from the Freie Universität Berlin has summarised the results of a study of the exercise and of the attitudes of the participants to micro-CHP and other novel energy technologies, like PV solar, as follows.

> Pioneers of fuel cell micro-CHP come from a well-educated, established middle class population with good income, though they are not the urban academic ecologists we found in the photovoltaic case, but rather a more rural and conservative group. Their education is very often of a technical nature, spurring interest in new technologies. What is striking is their relatively high age and the almost complete absence of women.

> As expected, they show a keen technical interest and environmental consciousness. They also combine the two: they hope to be able to solve environmental problems by means of technology. Both concerns converge in the notion of the 'forward-looking'. The pioneers trust in their own ability to solve problems, be they of a technical or environmental nature. Therefore, they want to make their own contribution. Many of them possess green energy technologies like solar heat or heat pump, or efficient household appliances. These technologies might serve as a 'door opener'.

> The pioneer's interest in fuel cell micro-CHP was spurred by an interest in environmental protection and the desire to be the first in testing a novelty spur. However, like everybody else, the pioneers demanded cost-effectiveness, reliability and user friendliness from their home energy system. The pioneers spotted the deficits in the units that needed to be addressed before launch onto the mass market. But they also had a value in their willingness to promote the new technology and function as communicators and multipliers. All of the pioneers were well established and respected home owners who were active in the community.'

In terms of what the study means for the role of users in the diffusion of energy innovation, the researchers conclude:

> It shows that pioneer users play an important role. First, by their willingness to risk the experiment with a novel, immature technology, test it, and give qualified feedback as to the deficits and development needs. Secondly, by their enthusiasm about sharing their experience and spreading the word by which they can open markets. It also shows that pioneers are a special group in some,

but not in all respects. Technology pioneers are not necessarily lifestyle pioneers, they need not be – and in this case, definitely are not – concerned with sufficiency issues or political ecology. They share the concerns of mainstream users with cost effectiveness and comfort, but are willing to put them aside for the sake of the experiment. In sharing these concerns, they build an important bridge to the mass market. In being willing to put them aside, they are the relevant multipliers and valuable partners technology developers need to make their products pass the reality test.

(Fischer, 2004)

4.4 Conclusions

Looking back at the examples covered in this section, it is clear that, if they want to, consumers can change the way their power is supplied, for example by getting PV solar arrays fitted on the roof or by having small generating systems of various types installed in their homes. The take-up of some ideas, like rooftop wind turbines, may currently be small, but the use of PV solar is spreading rapidly, albeit with grants and subsidies helping to offset its relatively high cost. As costs fall, it could well become a common feature. By contrast, the various new domestic-scale micropower plants are available at costs not too dissimilar to that of conventional gas boilers, and this technology could well diffuse into wide-scale usage.

A recent study for the Energy Saving Trust suggested that by 2050 micro-CHP could be supplying 40 per cent of UK domestic heating and, along with other micropower systems, around 25 per cent of electricity.

However, the take up of micropower units depends on the commitment of consumers. Certainly, this type of response is more radical than that covered in Section 3, which looked at examples where consumers simply changed to green energy suppliers. For most people, going further may seem too much bother. Nevertheless, as the next section will illustrate, even more radical responses can occasionally be made. In the examples in this section, the consumers were simply buying in systems provided by conventional companies. The next section looks at examples where consumers who were dissatisfied with what was on offer have developed new or improved technologies themselves.

Exercise 4　Factors influencing adoption of novel power systems

Assess the factors shaping the take-up of novel domestic-scale micropower systems looked at in this section, by consumers, using Rogers' classification of the factors influencing adoption, as outlined in Section 1.

Discussion

Clearly there is a tension between costs and environmental concern – only the most environmentally concerned consumers are likely to buy into new technologies like micro-wind, solar PV and micro-CHP if they are significantly more expensive than conventional systems. Moreover, in terms of Rogers' observability and trialability requirements, systems like this are still fairly novel, so not many people will have seen them or have experience of them in use. There may also be concerns about technical performance and reliability, as well as compatibility with existing systems and lifestyles. So it's likely to be an uphill struggle to get them accepted.

Nevertheless, as the technology improves, becoming more familiar and cheaper, and if consumer awareness of wider environmental problems of the existing technology increases, then the relative advantage of adopting new systems may become more apparent. This assessment may be further stimulated if the existing power supply system does not seem to offer reliable power, as appears to have been the case in parts of the USA in recent years. While some consumers with special environmental, operational or performance concerns may become innovators and early adopters of these new ideas, governments can stimulate diffusion by providing financial incentives to householders.

If you are near your computer or DVD player this is a good time to watch the video on 'Home power'.

Key points of Section 4

- Motivated consumers and enthusiasts may sometimes adopt radically new products and services when existing offerings are perceived as inadequate, unreliable or undesirable.

- Increasing environmental concerns and problems with reliability of energy supplies may lead more consumers to adopt radical new technologies, such as domestic-scale renewable energy systems for self-generation.

- These various types of proactive consumer responses may begin to change the market for energy and how energy is generated and used, stimulating the development and spread of new technologies.

The key points for Section 4 meet learning outcomes 1.2, 1.3 and 1.4.

5 Consumers innovate

5.1 Consumer developer

The focus in this section is on consumer involvement that goes beyond the adoption of existing products developed by companies. It looks at examples of proactive consumer approaches, where the development, diffusion and marketing of specific products is initiated by, and even sometimes carried out by, user groups, rather than by companies. The examples are, once again, drawn from the renewable energy field.

5.2 Grass-roots solar energy initiatives

solar clubs

self-help community organisations set up to help householders to install solar energy units in their homes

The first case study concerns initiatives by users and consumers in the UK in relation to solar energy powered heating systems. In the 1990s a dozen or so do-it-yourself solar clubs emerged around the country, run by people who wanted access to solar energy devices to install in their homes for water heating, but could not find what they needed, at least not cheaply, on the market. By forming a self-help solar club, a group of individuals can share skills, labour and purchasing power, thereby cutting costs and making DIY installation easier. The club may also be able to access information and possibly financial support from aid agencies. Once established, the clubs can pass on their experiences and expertise to new members. Several community organisations emerged to help support the spread of such clubs and attract funding.

Case study | Solar clubs

Solar clubs are community organisations set up to make it easier and cheaper for householders to install an active solar water-heating system. Club members develop and share new skills, and this expertise can be passed on to new members, with one important area of course being safety awareness.

In some cases club members have developed their own solar collector designs or modified existing designs but even when using off-the-shelf commercial collectors, by buying in plumbing and other associated materials in bulk and installing the collectors themselves they can reduce the total cost. In 2005 a solar collector fitted on a roof and plumbed into the central heating system cost between £1800 and £2000 if self-installed, and was expected to cut annual water heating bills in half.

The first clubs were set up in Bristol and Leicester, following the award of a two-year grant from the Environmental Action Fund to the Centre for Sustainable Energy (CSE) in partnership with Environ, in Leicester, in 1997. During this pilot period, over 100 members installed solar water-heating systems in the Bristol and Leicester areas. Then in 1998, when the BOC Foundation contributed extra funding, the programme expanded to support the launch of ten new solar clubs around the UK. Introductory seminars were held in Bristol and Leicester in 1999 to disseminate the findings of the pilot project, and to invite applications to set up clubs as part of the network.

By 2000 there were 13 solar self-help organisations around the UK, all operating on a not-for-profit basis, which means they do not take commission from sales of solar heating equipment to their members and that all savings made through discounts are passed on to the members of the clubs. Each club also offers a choice of at least three types of solar panel from manufacturers, all of whom are members of the UK's Solar Trade Association.

The idea has continued to spread around the country. For example, in 2001 the Milton Keynes-based National Energy Foundation set up Self Sol, a solar self-build support organisation, providing training for householders wishing to install solar devices. Similar groups have emerged in Wales, Yorkshire, Berkshire and many other places (Figure 15). In 2003 a Solar for London organisation emerged, growing out of a pioneering solar club, with support from the national Energy Saving Trust and the London-based campaign group Sustainable Energy Action. In parallel, a variety of local organisations around the country offer short solar installation training courses, following on from the pioneering work of the Centre for Alternative Technology in Wales.

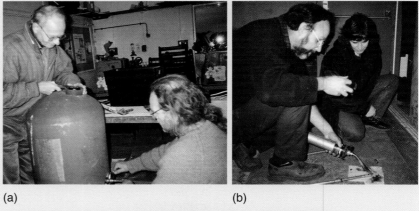

(a)   (b)

Figure 15 (a and b) Solar club training sessions in Wales

The solar heat collectors used did not involve radical innovation – the idea of rooftop solar collectors was well established. Instead the local users and enthusiasts adapted the concept to their needs. However, even if technological innovation may not have been the key element in the self-build solar club movement in the UK, the approach adopted to getting access to the technology and its subsequent diffusion was certainly innovative, via the creation of grass-roots networks to get access to technical support, cheap materials and to spread the idea.

The second case study concerns a grass-roots solar collector initiative in Austria, which started in the 1980s. This has been more innovative in terms of both the technology and building a market for it. In this initiative local activists developed a novel solar heat collector designed for DIY assembly. The development of the design was incremental, with feedback from early users being used to inform design changes. This process helped create a version which was taken up by 100 000 users, making Austria one of the leaders in the use of solar power – for water heating, but also in some situations for space heating. This led to the installation of 2 million square metres of solar heat collectors by the end of the 1990s, of which about 400 000 m^2 were self-build systems. Enthusiasm for the use of solar power in Austria, including self-built units, has continued since then. A survey in 2004 found that Austria was third in the world league of solar water heating users, on a per capita basis. Only Israel and Greece had more.

The T307 DVD contains a short section on the Austrian initiative (see the *Block 4 Guide*).

Case study | Solar energy diffusion in Austria

The following is an edited extract from a review of the experience with self-constructed solar water heating devices in Austria, by Michael Ornetzeder from the Zentrum für Soziale Innovation (Ornetzeder, 2001).

Two skilled Styrian amateur inventors, a fruit farmer and a technical engineer, initiated the Austrian successful dissemination of solar water heaters nearly 90 years after the first patent on this technology was taken out. Together with some friends, they developed a simple self-construction method adapted to the needs and abilities of the rural population. The first self-construction group with 32 participants was established in a small village near Graz in 1983. A few years later, the motives for this co-operation were summarised by the initiators as follows:

> Our primary aim was to build a collector that was inexpensive and easy to build for every one of us. Having become aware of the finiteness of natural resources, we also aimed at avoiding all material waste in constructing the collector. Other important aspects were the saving of energy, environmental protection, and community building. Everybody was expected to build their own collector in order to be sufficiently familiar with its function.

> (Hödl and Plesch, 1988)

The idea to practise do-it-yourself methods in a group was based on a local tradition. This rural part of Austria, eastern Styria, is well known for its wine and fruits. People of this countryside are used to co-operating, at least during harvest season. Even in a technical world, apples of high quality have to be picked manually. So, once a year, all available family members, friends and neighbours work together for a short time. The experience of organising and motivating an informal working-group could easily be transferred to other purposes.

The positive experiences of the first construction group were soon spread by word of mouth and fuelled the neighbouring communities' interest in utilising this new technology that tapped the sun's energy. Before the end of 1984, the enormous demand for these heaters required the establishment of two more construction groups, each with more than 100 participants. When more requests were made from other parts of eastern Styria, some of the more active know-how carriers decided to hold a series of evening lectures in order to report on the solar system self-construction method. These information lectures were usually organised by one of the people interested in building his or her own solar heater.

From 1986 onwards, the self-construction group leaders met on a monthly basis to discuss the advantages and drawbacks of different types of systems. They invited manufacturers to present their products, compared several offers and placed orders for several construction groups. Due to these bulk purchases, they were able to offer collectors at competitive prices. During that period, the technical system underwent a number of important improvements based upon practical feedback of former participants and technical skills of new group members. For instance, the piping of the absorber was no longer soldered at every bend but produced from a single piece of copper tube. For this purpose, a special tube-fitting table was developed (Figure 16). At the same time, the device used for soldering sheets and pipes was considerably improved.

Figure 16 Tube-fitting table in use in Austria. A continuous length of heat-absorbing copper pipe is being bent into a pattern. This technique avoids having to fit joints at each bend. Source: T307 DVD video

These two technical innovations brought not only manufacturing advantages but, by making soldering spots redundant, also a reduction in the finished system's susceptibility to break down. A further improvement was achieved with regard to the collector housing, which to prevent corrosion was no longer made of zinc-lined steel sheet but instead was of high-grade steel. In 1986, the first collectors that could be directly integrated into the house roof, if the tilt and orientation were suitable, became available. This installation method made it possible to cut financial expenses by avoiding the need for steel housing and, in many cases it improved the look of the collector.

The special tools that had been developed were made into a complete tool kit that was initially rented to other groups for a small fee. In 1986, the Styrian self-builders, based only in a small region, were able to produce more solar collector surface area than all the commercial suppliers in Austria put together (Figure 17).

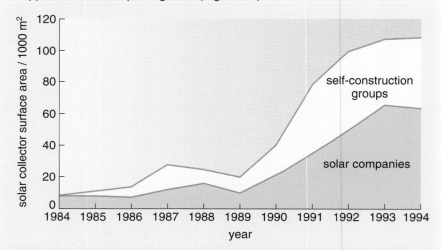

Figure 17 Solar collectors in Austria shown as the proportion installed by self-construction groups and by installation companies, 1984–1994 Source: Ornetzeder, 2001. Growth continued after 1994, although commercial units began to dominate, for example by the end of 1999 Austria had 2 000 000 m² of solar collectors installed of which about 400 000 m² were self-constructed

In order to meet the ever-increasing demand, in 1987 the first solar system build-it-yourself guide was produced. Training seminars were organised for construction group leaders and other interested persons who wanted to familiarise themselves with the method of solar system self-building. To improve communication, a news bulletin titled *Solar Info* was established.

An important step in this process was the institutionalisation of the self-construction movement. The Association for Renewable Energy (AEE) was founded in Gleisdorf in June 1988. The AEE was awarded several environmental and research prizes, which brought them additional recognition. As an official representative of the solar system self-construction movement, the AEE was able to receive public funds support. This enabled the AEE to do their work on both a broader and more stable basis. After a few years, the AEE expanded throughout Austria by establishing regional divisions. The self-construction method also found followers in neighbouring countries such as Switzerland, the Czech Republic, Slovakia and Slovenia.

As a result of increasing demand on solar systems for space heating, some important improvements were made. An even more efficient type of collector was developed, and the usage of commercially available selective absorber strips was enabled. The AEE became, meanwhile, one of the most important know-how carriers not only in the field of thermal solar energy but also in regard to other renewables in Austria. Nevertheless, in spite of these recent developments, the organisational culture of the AEE still resembles that of a social movement.

Atypical inventors

This case study shows that new technology can be successful in niches, which may at first sight seem rather unusual.

The solar adopters in Austria do not fit Rogers' category of innovators – not only do they not have the demographic characteristics associated with innovators, but they have also played a large part in the development of the technology. Instead they can be characterised as atypical innovators.

Who were the Austrian adopters? Research shows they had an average age of approximately 40 years, younger than the average population. More than half of them had completed a middle-level education, for instance at a further education college. Household incomes tended to be lower than average and solar collectors were installed mainly in larger households, with an average size of more than four persons – an average Austrian household consists of only 2.5 persons and this number is decreasing.

The most remarkable characteristic of the adopters was the extraordinary proportion of farmers and part-time farmers, nearly 50 per cent in Styria and Lower Austria, and 31 per cent in Upper Austria. There are several reasons for this atypical group of adopters. On farms there is normally a higher demand for warm water: a private and an operational one. Farmhouses are usually big enough, so there is no problem with the installation of a solar system. Beyond this, most of these houses were equipped with old heating technology. In summer people had to heat these systems every day in order to receive hot water.

A solar system therefore means a lot of added comfort. In Styria, as well as in Lower Austria, 'added comfort' was in fact the most important motivation to adopt a solar system (Figure 18). The individual's perceived advantage of more personal comfort was mainly stimulated by the obsolete heating equipment. In other words, old technology was a major precondition for the successful dissemination of solar heaters in these rural regions.

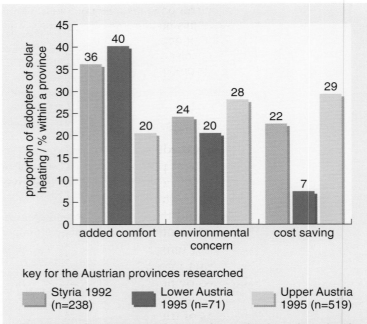

key for the Austrian provinces researched

■ Styria 1992 (n=238)   ■ Lower Austria 1995 (n=71)   ■ Upper Austria 1995 (n=519)

Figure 18 Comparison of the main motivations for adopting a solar heating system. The motivations were added comfort, environmental concern and cost saving. Research was done in the provinces of Lower Austria, Upper Austria, and Styria. Source: Ornetzeder, 2001

Conclusion

A central idea of diffusion theory, the perceived 'relative advantage' (Rogers, 1983), helps to explain the success of solar water heaters. An innovation spreads if it is perceived as superior to the product it replaces. The individual advantages of solar heaters (labour-saving, personal comfort) were first seen in the emergence of the technology in the United States as well as during the spread in Austria, an aspect of major importance. But the perception of an innovation as having relative advantage also depends on variable conditions. In the Austrian case, the new solar technology profited substantially from old heating systems in rural households.

The spreading of innovations usually leads to important technical optimisations, which add to the attractiveness of the original innovation. The Austrian self-construction movement could be seen as a large, decentralised development division for solar heating systems, in which over many years a great number of technical improvements were implemented. A great number of users all over Austria were and still are in contact with the AEE. Within this network of qualified users, positive and negative experiences with the technology are communicated. Users are close to the technology and some of them are directly involved in the improvement of systems. Many of these improvements have been adopted by commercial producers and installation companies – for example, a special glass cover sealing, using components from available glasshouse systems, and solar systems for space heating. In Austria, commercial solar systems are of good quality and prices are much lower than ten years ago.

Contrary to misgivings of solar companies, the success of the self-construction movement had positive effects on their sales as well. The further development of the solar market had an increasing dynamic by a self-enforcing process. A growing number of solar collectors made it easier for potential adopters to visit existing devices. More information about this new technology spread; people were more likely to have a friend or acquaintance who already had a solar heating system. In recent years solar companies have been successful in Austria, partly because of this precondition.

5.2.1 Grass-roots marketing

As the preceding case study illustrates, local user and consumer involvement provided not just a way of developing these new renewable energy technologies effectively, but also of marketing them. A study by the Austrian Academy of Sciences in 1996, entitled Express Path, found that, in most cases the initial innovation 'was spread by word of mouth in social movements or by communication processes in formal or informal networks of actors'. In particular, the most important marketing tool was said to be word-of-mouth promotion by satisfied owners of solar systems. About 60 per cent of those working in do-it-yourself groups became interested because of the existing systems of friends and neighbours.

On the innovation process the Academy's report notes:

> It was particularly interesting that in the first phase it was neither academic research, nor research within big enterprises, that led to successful prototypes that started diffusion. In all successful examples of diffusion it was either a grass-roots movement or small and medium enterprises that developed the first working prototypes. In all cases well working equipment was only obtained after several years and many examples of trial and error under normal operation conditions – and not in a laboratory. A close feedback between technology developers and technology users is critical in the early development phase. This means that maintenance and trouble shooting should be done by the producers to gain know-how on the critical points for reliable operation.

> A good example of failure is the first phase of the development of solar water heaters in Austria. This development was started by an ambitious initiative of federal government involving academic research institutions and large publicly owned metal industries. Collector systems that resulted from these efforts were sophisticated but too complicated and consequently expensive and not reliable in operation. Industry was neither able to supply appropriate maintenance services nor to change the design of the collectors flexibly. They produced large stocks that were useless when the market crashed. Only small firms survived this crash, which was operating on a rather localised level, with close contacts to customers.

> (Austrian Academy of Sciences, 1996)

SAQ 3

What advantages did the grass-roots Austrian solar collector innovators have over conventional corporate innovators?

SAQ 4

In terms of Rogers' classification of types of adopters as outlined in Section 1, how did the Austrian solar collector innovators differ from the energy consumers in California who adopted PV solar?

5.3 Danish wind power initiative

The UK and Austrian solar heat collector examples concerned relatively simple technology, with relatively straightforward incremental improvements being made to a familiar concept, involving incremental modifications and adaptation rather than radical innovation. However, as the next case study will illustrate, there are also examples of grass-roots inventors and user groups coming up with significant innovations involving more sophisticated technologies.

In the late 1970s in Denmark, local enthusiasts, amateur engineers and crafts people, in response to environmental concerns, began to develop small wind turbines for their own use, for instance on farms. They started with some existing small Danish wind turbine designs and then improved the designs on a piecemeal, incremental basis, until, by the early 1980s they had a robust technology. This was taken up by newly emerging turbine companies such as Vestas and Bonus who became world leaders, selling large numbers of turbines. This led to Denmark becoming a world leader in the wind turbine field. By 2003, 21 per cent of Danish electricity came from wind turbines and Denmark led the world in wind technology exports.

The early success of the grass-roots-initiated Danish wind programme was helped by small grants from the government and the creation of local initiatives. Most of the wind projects were owned by local people, through local wind co-operatives, who used the power and benefited from sales of any extra power fed to the national power grid. Around 80 per cent of the wind projects in Denmark are owned by individuals or local co-operative Wind Guilds, formed by the community. These locally owned projects have been much more successful than the utility company schemes (Figure 19).

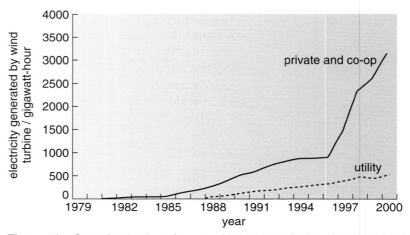

Figure 19 Growth of privately owned or co-op wind projects and utility-owned wind projects in Denmark Source: Elliott, 2003

The co-ops can be large; some have hundreds of members. Co-operatives have even been involved with some offshore projects (Figure 20). The co-ops have helped create and sustain a strong domestic market, which has provided a base for successful exports, and continued innovation.

Figure 20   The Middelgrunden offshore wind farm is just off the Danish coast, and is 50 per cent owned by a local residents' co-op Source: Lokefilm

In the late 1970s and early 1980s Danish grass-roots groups were incrementally improving small turbines with a 10–100-kilowatt capacity. At the same time, in the USA, and subsequently the UK, the emphasis was on large, multi-megawatt, high-tech wind turbines (remember 1 megawatt is 1000 kilowatts). These were developed by companies like Boeing and by NASA in the USA (the 2-MW Mod 2 series), and British Aerospace in the UK (the 3-MW Wind Energy Group machine on the Orkneys). The large machines proved to be too complex and expensive, and the giant prototypes have all since been abandoned, some after breakdowns. For example, the 3-MW Wind Energy Group machine on the Orkneys, which had cost £17 million to build, was shut down in 1992 after cracks were found in the hub section of the blades, and it was later demolished.

The Danish machines by comparison were much simpler and more robust, and the Danish programme was far less expensive. The Danish wind industry received a total of $52 million via government grants during the initial development phase, while the equivalent figure for the USA was $450 million. Moreover the machines that emerged were the right scale for the emerging market, and the Danish companies were well placed to use the market that had been built up from the grass-roots in Denmark as a springboard. Initially Denmark captured 90 per cent of the US wind turbine market.

Interestingly, in the years since this early phase, as other developers have joined the market, the scale of Danish wind turbines has gradually increased. The experience gained from small turbine development was built upon until robust multi-megawatt machines were created. Incremental development seems to have been the right approach for this technology.

The T307 DVD has a video on the renewable energy projects that have been adopted on the Danish island of Samsø. The projects include major onshore and offshore wind farms, part owned by local people (see the *Block 4 Guide*).

5.3.1 Grass-roots innovators

Innovation analyst Boru Douthwaite, whose work was mentioned in Section 1, is critical of what he called the over-the-wall approach to innovation that pays little attention to consumers' concerns. In the following extract he describes the Danish wind initiative with positive language, highlighting how grass-roots innovators successfully passed through the various stages of the innovation process, from creating novel ideas through to selecting improvements and then on to diffusion:

> A grass-roots development process in Denmark was able to produce a wind turbine industry with a 55% share of a billion dollar a year world market, beating the US who spent over 300 million dollars funding a top-down development program led by the National Aeronautics and Space Administration (NASA). The origins of the Danish industry were a few agricultural machinery manufacturers and ideologically motivated 'hobbyists' who began building, owning, and tinkering with wind turbines (generating novelty). There were many early teething problems but the owners organized themselves into a group who lobbied successfully for design improvements (selection), working closely with manufacturers to solve the problems. The owners' group developed a cooperative ownership model and pressured politicians to support the sale of their electricity to the national grid at a fair price (promulgation and diffusion). In contrast, the NASA led a top-down science development approach that implicitly assumed that scientists could develop the 'perfect' wind turbine with little input from the owners and users. NASA's approach failed.
>
> (Douthwaite, 2002b)

5.4   From the grass-roots to commercial success

The grass-roots initiatives by the Danish wind turbine innovators and the Austrian solar collector innovators both involved an interaction between product innovation and market diffusion. In both examples, there was a combination of incremental grass-roots technological and design activity, and the creation of a new and expanding market for the product. Technical innovation and market creation worked together in the development of new products.

In both cases the initial grass-roots innovation and marketing process has led to wider diffusion. The self-build solar initiative in Austria has helped create a national market for the technology. The grass-roots Danish wind turbines initiative had an even larger impact. It led to commercial success on an international scale. The small companies that were formed to develop the wind turbines have expanded to become major national and international players; they are now conventional businesses. By 2004 the Danish wind industry employed more than

20 000 people and had an annual turnover of over 3 billion euro (around £2 billion), with exports accounting for over 80 per cent of output.

Germany subsequently followed the Danish lead, with a domestic market secured by extensive local ownership of projects and by favourable subsidy arrangements, which laid the basis for rapidly expanding exports. In 1999, the European Wind Energy Association commented 'in some countries wind energy growth rates exceed the expansion of the mobile phone market'. Since then expansion has continued even more rapidly.

To varying degrees, the two examples of solar and wind in this section link to the sixth level of consumer involvement. The products discussed have gone from niche markets created by proactive consumers, to become part of the mainstream business market. However, in both cases there is still some continuing grass-roots involvement. In Austria, the local networks of users continue to provide advice and support, and in Denmark the wind co-operatives remain as a key part of the domestic market. So even though the overall trend has been towards the creation of conventional commercial businesses, there are still some grass-roots links, with important local market implications.

However, these bottom-up innovation and diffusion initiatives have to be put in context. At present, proactive grass-roots initiatives like this only involve a minority, for instance there are only 100 000 wind co-operative members in Denmark out of a population of 5 million, and direct grass-roots involvement in the innovation process, as opposed to the subsequent diffusion process, involved only a small number of people. Moreover, not every group of enthusiasts is going to come up with a world-beating idea. Most successful innovation still originates from conventional businesses, which have the necessary skills, expertise and finance to carry out development work and support effective diffusion. Nevertheless, as you will see in the next section, there are examples of significant bottom-up innovation and diffusion that have occurred in contexts where high levels of technological expertise were needed.

SAQ 5

To what extent did the examples of proactive consumer initiatives discussed in this section involve radical product invention?

Key points of Section 5

- Some consumers or users may have special needs and/or concerns, and, if the market does not provide what they feel is needed, they may act independently to develop new or improved products.

- Consumers or users can develop new or improved products and may sometimes help support wide diffusion of the ideas, which may lead to the creation of new markets.

- Proactive consumer or user groups, adopting a craft level and almost DIY approach, have developed a range of novel products in the renewable energy field, some of which have diffused widely and been commercially successful.

- As it provides more opportunity for interaction with users, iterative feedback and incremental evolution, the grass-roots bottom-up approach can sometimes be more successful than the conventional top-down corporate approach in terms of delivering viable products that meet people's needs in environmentally and socially appropriate ways.

The key points for Section 5 meet learning outcomes 1.2, 1.3 and 1.4.

6 Consumers, producers and pressure groups

6.1 Consumers as innovators

The emphasis in the previous section was on initiatives started at the grass-roots by people who had specific technical requirements – for wind turbines or solar collectors. This section explores whether the grass-roots, user-orientated approach can be relevant in other more conventional areas of technology. The examples include initiatives by consumers, users and other interested parties, such as pressure groups that have access to significant technical expertise, coupled with special enthusiasms and/or concerns.

But whatever the starting point these consumer-orientated innovations diffuse and become part of the mainstream market.

6.2 Bottom-up initiatives in computing

Novel ideas often come from technological enthusiasts. Apple Computer is a prime example. In 1976 two young Californian computer enthusiasts, members of their local Homebrew Computer Club, developed a cheap personal computer, designed initially to be sold as a DIY self-assembly kit in the hobbyist market. They set up a small company and began production in a garage owned by one of their parents. They then moved on to develop an innovative desktop machine. This helped the company expand rapidly. By 1980 it had a net income of $61 million rising to $583 million by 1982.

Apple's fortunes improved even more following the adoption of the icon-and-windows concept that had initially been developed, but not followed up, by Xerox. Apple used this system in the Macintosh personal computer (Mac for short) launched in 1984. The emphasis was on a user-friendly approach; Macs were designed to be easy to use by novices.

Subsequently, the PC market expanded, and machines from other companies emerged that made use of the icon-and-windows concept. Apple continued to be innovative and went on to develop the well-received iMac and iBook. Although Apple has a small percentage of the domestic computer market, Apple machines are widely used by professionals in the design and graphics world and they have around 30 per cent of the education market.

From the early initiatives of two consumer innovators, Steve Jobs and Steve Wozniack, Apple has grown to become a conventional, international company. However, the grass-roots approach to computer system development has continued. For example, there is an extensive hobbyist movement of people who build customised computers, often of novel design, using basic components bought from specialist retailers.

In the development of software, Linux computer software provides an example of a major bottom-up innovation. In this case enthusiasts created a unique and popular operating system, which has been continually refined by users, through the exchange of ideas on the internet. These enthusiasts have tried to create an alternative to the dominant Microsoft software using the enthusiasm, skills and knowledge of programmers and users who offered to give their time for free to help users like themselves. This approach is sometimes called open source software development, and is an extension of the free access shareware idea. (Box 4 has more about Linux.)

Box 4   Linux operating system

Boru Douthwaite describes the Linux initiative as follows:

'[An] example of the power that a grass-roots innovation model can harness is the development of the computer operating system Linux, which is a "a world-class operating system" that has coalesced "as if by magic out of part-time hacking by several thousand developers all over the planet connected only by the tenuous strands of the Internet" (Raymond, 1997).

'Linux started life when a Finnish computer science student [Linus Torvalds] started to write a Unix-like operating system that he could run on his PC; he had become tired of having to queue for hours to gain access to Unix on the University's mainframe. When he finally got the core of an operating system working he posted it on the Internet so that others could try it out. Importantly he gave the source code so other people could understand the program and modify it if they wanted. Just like the first Danish wind turbines, early versions of Linux were not technically sophisticated or elegant, but they were simple, understandable, and touched a chord with "hackers", people like Torvalds himself who got a kick out of generating novelty for the sake of being creative, not for money.

'Torvalds' main role in the development of Linux after the first release was not to write code for features people wanted but to select and propagate improvements to the system from the ideas that streamed in. Ten people downloaded version 0.02 and five of these sent him bug fixes, code improvements and new features. Torvalds added the best of these to the existing program along with others he had written himself and released the composite as version 0.12. The rate of learning selection accelerated as the number of users increased, and to cope with the volume of hacks (novelties) coming in, Torvalds began choosing and relying on a type of peer review. Rather than evaluate every modification himself he based his decisions on the recommendation of people he trusted and on whether people were already using the patch (modification) successfully. He in fact played a similar role to that of an editor of an academic journal who makes sure submitted articles are reviewed but retains final control over what is published and what is not. This approach has allowed Torvalds to keep the program on track as it has grown from 10 000 lines of code to 1.5 million, all written by volunteers.'

(Douthwaite, 2002b)

This bottom-up approach has been successful. A Microsoft engineer commented, 'The ability of the open source software process to collect and harness the collective IQ of thousands of individuals across the Internet is simply amazing.' As a result, Linux became a quite widely used system. Although it could not compete with Microsoft for general PC use, by 1998 it was installed on 17 per cent of servers, the computers that run networks including the internet. Since then, although the software remains free – the basic Linux source code is openly available to all users – it has been the basis for commercial spin-offs from companies like Red Hat, which soon after its launch in 1999 was worth $15 billion (Douthwaite, 2002a).

Not everyone involved with creating Linux is happy with the trend towards commercialisation; some see it as using Linux to sell expensive computer services and systems and restricting free access to Linux. Linux activist Bruce Perens, co-founder of the Open Source Initiative, commented in the January 2004 issue of the IT journal *Information Age*, 'We, the free software developers, created this software to empower everyone, and for everyone to share.'

The Linux software has also been used by an Indian company, Amida, which launched the Simputer, a 64-Mbyte, portable microcomputer in 2004. The free software helps to keep the cost low (around $240) and makes the computer easy to use, offering good connectivity to the internet and a wider range of peripherals. The Simputer has a touch screen rather than a keyboard and can accept hand-written text in a variety of languages, ideal for beginners. The computer was developed by a not-for-profit trust, and manufacturing franchises have been offered widely to assist diffusion. The product is seen by the manufacturers as helping to overcome the 'digital divide' between those who have computers and those who don't.

The approach adopted by those who created Linux may seem altruistic, especially given the fact that the product has gone on to make money for shareholders and investors in computer companies who have used Linux as a basis for their business – by selling hardware and ancillary software. However, as one observer noted, most of the people initially involved with Linux were 'hackers' who were not 'classically economic', given that they mostly had good jobs already; instead they were motivated by 'their own ego satisfaction and reputation among other hackers'.

Not everyone is in a position to challenge large corporations in this way, not least because only a few will have the necessary technical expertise. Although operating independently, some of those involved with the creation of Linux had jobs in the computer industry or were freelance experts. So in some areas of information technology, the distinction between 'insiders' who have expertise and are employed by businesses, and 'outsiders' without expertise is beginning to break down.

The distinction between producers (as insiders) and consumers (as outsiders) may also be breaking down, particularly when it comes to issues of sustainability. Both producers and consumers will be affected by the environmental impact of their decisions. The next subsection explores some of the ways in which producers can influence which technologies should be developed and how they should be developed, even if that is outside their specific job role.

6.3 Producers as independent innovators

The new sensitivity about the nature of technological development is not just limited to people in their role as consumers. While only a few consumers get involved directly with creating innovation, for many designers and engineers innovation is the focus of their job. Company innovation like this was the focus of the earlier course material. Ideas may also come from other employees within a company; many companies collect ideas via such schemes as suggestion boxes, though often suggestions are focused on process innovation rather than product innovation.

However, there have been examples where producers have taken an active role, outside their job. For example, some trade union groups were among the pioneers of the idea of shifting to socially and environmentally appropriate production. In the UK in the 1970s trade unionists at Lucas Aerospace argued that rather than having to rely on defence-related production, job security could be better ensured by shifting to socially needed products and systems, and they developed their own plan outlining 150 new products which they felt they should work on. These included wind turbines, solar energy devices and fuel cells, as well as medical equipment. Several other trade union groups in the UK subsequently developed similar plans, as did some labour organisations in the USA.

These early initiatives were at a time when the idea of sustainable technology, based on renewable energy and environmental protection, was in its infancy, and in most cases the companies concerned repressed or ignored the plans that emerged from their workforces. Indeed some of the activists involved in the UK were dismissed for challenging the management's right to choose what to produce. While there is still little acceptance of workers' rights to participate in decision-making, some of the technical ideas that emerged from these early campaigns are now more respectable, and many companies are keen to be seen to be green.

Trade unions in the UK have continued to press for environmentally sound production, and there are some interesting workplace initiatives designed to help producers explore the environmental implications of what they do at work and consider alternative options. One example is the web-based Environmental Practice at Work facility (see **www.epaw.co.uk**).

The interesting aspect of workplace-based initiatives is that those involved can often bring to the discussion of 'what to make' extensive knowledge of the needs of their local community, as well as an understanding of the limits and opportunities of production systems.

6.4 Role of designers: design for need

Over the years the design profession has shown increasing interest in what Victor Papanek called 'design for the real world', which is the title of his influential book published in 1972. Decades later his words remain relevant when he argues that,

> Much recent design has satisfied only evanescent wants and desires, while the genuine needs of man have often been neglected by the

designer. The economic, psychological, spiritual, technological and intellectual needs of a human being are usually more difficult and less profitable to satisfy than the carefully engineered and manipulated 'wants' inculcated by fad and fashion ...

(Papanek, 1972)

In subsequent years some designers attempted to focus on meeting human needs more effectively, particularly working on the development of aids for people with disabilities. In the UK around 18 per cent of the working-age population has some form of disability, and due to demographic changes, by 2020 around 50 per cent of the adult population will be 50 or over, so there will be an increasing demand for technologies that take account of the special needs of older people. You saw some examples of this 'inclusive design' in the *Markets* block.

Other designers responded to Papanek's work by focusing on what is sometimes called intermediate technology, meaning technologies appropriate to the needs of people in newly developing countries.

However, important though it is to those involved, meeting special needs like these is a small fraction of design activity and one that comes about mainly because of altruistic, ethical and humanitarian commitments.

The development of environmentally friendly products and systems has sometimes been seen in a similar way as worthy but not central to the economy. But as awareness of the scale of the global environmental problems like climate change has grown, it has been realised that the development of environmentally safe technologies are no longer an optional extra but a matter of urgent necessity. The social and economic impacts of problems like climate change are likely to be global, affecting the survival of everyone on the planet. So it is not surprising that there has been increasing interest in sustainable energy technology in recent years. Designers are now faced with the technological and environmental challenges of working on green energy projects and designing green products and services.

6.5   Role of pressure groups

In this block you have travelled in a circle in terms of the involvement of consumers and the initiation of innovation. In the first few sections you looked at conventional business approaches, where the consumer simply made choices from the offerings of producers. You then looked at consumers who were slightly less passive. Subsequent sections looked at the more radical involvement of consumers and users. Some operated outside of the conventional system but some crossed the line to become producers. Section 6 has looked at mainstream companies where people have had some kind of internal, radical involvement.

There is, however, another level of influence external to companies that needs to be discussed. Some large organisations have grown up to inform and protect the consumer and others have grown up with a similar brief for the environment. Pressure groups have also emerged to press for changes on certain issues. These organisations and pressure groups are exerting increasing influence on which technologies are developed and how they evolve. This section therefore concludes the discussion of consumer involvement with a brief look at the role that pressure groups can play in influencing the innovation and diffusion efforts of conventional companies.

There is no shortage of examples of consumer or environmental campaigns against the products and activities of business – such campaigns can be effective. Some of the more effective pressure group campaigns have focused on positive alternatives. One example is the campaign mounted by the international environmental pressure group Greenpeace for renewable energy technologies like PV solar and offshore wind. Greenpeace has worked closely with the relevant industries, including, in the case of PV solar, some oil companies with whom they have previously been in conflict in other areas of the companies' work. The aim of their campaign is to try to bring about a redirection of corporate effort.

Consumer and environmental pressure groups can attract support from large numbers of people and can attract widespread attention for their views via the media. Consumers have increasingly begun to take notice of information provided by such organisations and to exert consumer power collectively. As markets have globalised, so has consumer power. International environmental groups and ethical trading schemes can create a consumer backlash against companies who transgress, and the response can be huge and instantaneous when the internet is used to mobilise public opinion.

This is not always a negative reaction; organisations are also increasingly trying to stimulate demand for environmentally friendly products and services, and sometimes such initiatives find support from large numbers of consumers.

An example of a positive development is the Greenfreeze ozone-friendly refrigerator, developed in the early 1990s with support from Greenpeace. Its development illustrates the way in which outsider groups can have a significant impact on the innovation and diffusion process.

In 1987 an international protocol was signed (the Montreal protocol) to reduce the use of chlorofluorocarbons (CFCs) as coolants in fridges and in other uses, because when these gases are released into the atmosphere they damage the ozone layer, which protects the Earth from dangerous wavelengths of solar radiation. Subsequent negotiations led to agreements to phase out the use of CFCs entirely. The refrigeration industry favoured the use of hydrofluorocarbons (HFCs) as a replacement for CFCs. However, Greenpeace argued this option was flawed because HFCs play a role in climate change. Instead Greenpeace proposes the use of hydrocarbon gases – either a mixture of propane and isobutane, or isobutane as a pure gas. Although these gases are flammable, Greenpeace saw them as a better option than HFCs.

The idea of using hydrocarbons had been suggested and tested by two medical doctors at the Dortmund Institute of Hygiene, who, as well as being worried about the atmospheric impacts of the industry's chosen gases, were also concerned about possible toxic impacts. Their ideas were picked up by Greenpeace, who supported the development of the

Greenfreeze concept by DKK Scharfenstein (later to be called Foron). This company was a refrigerator manufacturer based in East Germany.

Following the reunification of Germany, Foron was threatened with closure. In 1992 Greenpeace provided $17 000 for the construction of ten prototypes – initially under the name of Clean Cooler – and acted as a product champion and advocate. It defended the idea strongly against the initial opposition of most of the rest of the refrigerator manufacturing industry, which argued that using flammable hydrocarbons was dangerous and the system would not be energy efficient.

Greenpeace publicised and promoted the idea through its extensive network of members and supporters. Through Greenpeace's grass-roots publicity activities and product endorsement over 100 000 orders for the new product were generated in less than a year.

The commercial success of Greenfreeze in Germany, and the discovery that hydrocarbons performed better than the industry had expected, led the conventional manufacturers to develop their own versions. By 1994 all German refrigerator manufacturers either had switched to Greenfreeze technology or were planning to convert. Since then the technology has become widely used across the EU.

Greenpeace was clearly able to support both technical innovation and widespread diffusion. However, the organisation was careful not to be seen as allied to any one company – its aim was to promote improved technology not specific companies. (Box 5 has more about this.).

Greenpeace saw its involvement as a creative way to deal with environmental problems, and said that it would be happy to 'create new alliances with sectors such as businesses and industries' to support similar projects. Subsequently, following up this commitment, Greenpeace backed the Juice green power retail scheme set up by npower. As noted in Section 3, this made use of power from the company's new offshore wind farm at North Hoyle off the coast of North Wales, which was commissioned in 2003 and by 2004 Juice had 40 000 subscribers.

Box 5 Greenfreeze

Greenpeace recounts the story as follows:

> In the spring of 1992, Greenpeace brought together scientists who had extensively researched the use of propane and butane as refrigerants, with an East German company DKK Scharfenstein. The company had been producing refrigerators for 50 years and was the leading household appliance manufacturer in the former East Germany. However, after reunification, it faced severe economic problems and was due to be closed down.
>
> The meeting between the scientists and DKK Scharfenstein resulted in the birth of Greenfreeze technology for domestic refrigeration. Greenfreeze refrigerators use hydrocarbons for both the blowing of the insulation foam and the refrigerant and they are entirely free of ozone destroying and global warming chemicals. When DKK Scharfenstein announced its intention to mass-produce Greenfreeze, Greenpeace successfully campaigned to gather tens of thousands of preorders for the yet-to-be-produced

new refrigerator, from environmentally conscious consumers in Germany. This overwhelming support from the public secured the capital investment needed for the new Greenfreeze product, and at the same time, salvaged the company and saved the jobs of its workers.

The major household appliance manufacturers, which had already invested in HFC-134a refrigeration technology as the substitute for CFCs, at first claimed that the Greenfreeze concept would not work. However, upon realizing that the first completely CFC, HCFC and HFC-free refrigerator was about to come on the market, and recognizing the market appeal of a truly environmentally friendly refrigerator, the four biggest producers, Bosch, Siemens, Liebherr and Miele, gave up their resistance to the hydrocarbon technology, and introduced their own line of Greenfreeze models in the spring of 1993.

Within a year and a half the Greenfreeze technology has spread like wildfire throughout Europe, and to other parts of the world. Many models of Greenfreeze refrigerators are now on sale in Germany, Austria, Denmark, France, Italy, Netherlands, Switzerland, and the UK. All of the major European companies, Bosch, Siemens, Electrolux, Liebherr, Miele, Quelle, Vestfrost, Bauknecht, Foron, AEG, are marketing Greenfreeze-technology-based refrigerators. Even the environmental ministers of Britain, Denmark and the Netherlands have lent their support by buying a Greenfreeze refrigerator.

(Greenpeace, undated)

6.6 Conclusion

As this section has illustrated, 'outsider' individuals, groups and organisations do seem to be able to have some influence on the innovation and diffusion process even in areas of complex technology. Some initiatives like Linux clearly have had a significant technological impact and those involved have tried to ensure the basic user-orientated values and bottom-up approach have been sustained, despite pressure for co-option by commercial interests. This section also looked at the role that pressure groups can play in influencing the innovation and diffusion efforts of conventional companies.

As with many of the case studies you looked at earlier in this block, the examples here illustrate once again the close interaction between new product development and subsequent diffusion. Greenpeace's intervention in both aspects was crucial to the success of Greenfreeze, and the successful spread of Linux was due to the direct engagement of its initiators in the user community. The same could be said in relation to the early history of Apple Macintosh computers.

The other main common factor in the examples in this section is that although they were all bottom-up, in the sense of mostly being initiated by outsiders of various sorts, the innovative initiatives involved a high level of technological expertise, and some led subsequently to direct engagement with conventional businesses, or the creation of new businesses. Either way, they all led on to successful products, widely adopted in the marketplace.

As was illustrated in this section and in the *Products* block, similar ideas are emerging from within companies, for example when company designers meet the challenge of developing sustainable technologies.

What is unclear is whether examples like the Greenfreeze fridge and Linux, or even Apple Macs, are one-offs, or whether these trends are more significant and affect mainstream innovation as carried out by conventional companies. Though the views of pressure groups are important, they cannot become the main source of independent authority on which technology is developed, especially as such groups often have conflicting perspectives and agendas. Moreover, there is another important guardian of environmental and consumer interests – the government. The next section looks at how governments try to influence technological developments and stimulate diffusion of desired technological options.

SAQ 6

Innovations created by proactive consumers are a rare thing. Isn't most innovation carried out by large teams in companies?

Key points of Section 6

- Bottom-up initiatives can lead to new product developments in complex areas of technology – including information technology.

- Outsiders can develop new product ideas which may form the basis of successful new businesses.

- The bottom-up approach may lead to products that are more user friendly.

- Pressure groups can play a positive role in the innovation and diffusion process, for example by stimulating the development of environmentally appropriate technologies and supporting their diffusion.

The key points for Section 6 meet learning outcomes 1.2 and 1.3.

7 Government and sustainable energy

7.1 Innovation and the government

Governments have always played a role in the innovation process, most notably in defence-related technology because historically one area of key responsibility is the 'defence of the realm' against external threats. Governments have also supported the development of other technologies felt to be of strategic economic and national importance, on the basis that the state can take a longer-term view than the private sector, and can raises taxes to pay for projects that are in the wider public interest.

Emphasis in the past has been on large government-funded R&D programmes and projects, carried out by state-controlled organisations, or in universities. However, in recent decades the emphasis around the world has moved towards a market-led approach, with governments intervening mainly to support, but also regulate, the activities of the private sector.

I will move on from the bottom-up approaches explored in previous sections to consider a top-down approach. In this section I will look at how governments can ensure the successful development and spread of strategically selected technologies. This will include a look at new technology development as well as at diffusion because the successful diffusion of new products frequently rests on how well those products have been developed.

To see how this process operates, you will examine the UK government's response to the threat of climate change, an 'external threat' of major proportions. The huge potential cost of climate change has compelled most governments to take some action. Launching an international Roundtable discussion meeting of the G8 industrial nations in November 2004, the UK Prime Minister Tony Blair commented:

> Over the coming decades, a massive shift towards lower carbon energy systems will be needed if we are to meet the world's growing energy needs whilst also avoiding the worst impacts of climate change. To achieve this, we will need a green technological revolution.

In response, the UK government called for the UK's carbon dioxide emissions to be reduced by 20 per cent by 2010 and 60 per cent by 2050 (both as compared with 1990 levels) and has established a range of polices and programmes to try to achieve these targets.

However, climate change does not have to be seen solely as a threat. Responding to it could be seen as offering opportunities for *sustainable* economic development. For example, the UK government's 2003 innovation review identified environmental issues, and the need for improved, lower impact products and services, as a key driver for future innovation. The review suggested that some of the new developments would be specific environmental goods and services, such as technologies to minimise pollutants or promote resource efficiency, or renewable energy sources.

In a follow-up report in 2005, *Securing the Future*, the government reinforced its commitment to supporting 'innovation for a sustainable future', and pointed out there was a global market worth over $500 billion for developments in this area.

7.2 Government energy policy options

Greenhouse gases are generated by many sectors, including the transport sector. However, to follow on from the case studies in previous sections, I will focus on the power supply sector.

There are many possible options for reducing greenhouse gas emissions such as carbon dioxide from the electricity generation process. One solution is to capture and store the carbon dioxide gas in undersea strata – this is called carbon sequestration. Other approaches are to increase energy efficiency in generation and use; to use lower carbon fuels like natural gas in power plants (fuel switching); and to switch to non-fossil fuels (renewables or nuclear).

These options all have their positive and negative aspects. For example, switching to natural gas reduces emissions, but gas reserves are limited, so this is only an interim solution. Similarly there is only limited room in secure undersea strata for storing captured emissions. Nuclear power plants do not generate carbon dioxide directly, but producing the fuel for them does, and they also produce dangerous and long-lived wastes. Renewable energy projects like wind farms are not limited in this way but they can be visually intrusive, and some renewable energy sources are intermittent or cyclical – wind is intermittent and tides are cyclical. So there is a range of strategic and tactical decisions to be made about which options to follow up and how much effort to put behind developing them.

Some of these technologies might eventually be adopted due to normal market pressures driven by the desire to save money as fossil fuel prices increase, as is likely in the longer term. When the UK electricity industry was privatised in 1990, there was a dramatic switch from coal to gas as a fuel for power stations because it was a cheaper option. However, new technologies may not always be cheaper initially, and new technologies usually take time to challenge well-established technologies. As the need for change is seen as urgent, governments have had to intervene.

7.3 Support options

There are various economic and administrative tools available to governments to promote the development and adoption of new technologies. Some penalise those who continue to use 'dirty' technologies, others reward those who adopt clean technologies.

Broadly the key tools can be grouped as follows:

- regulation – setting and policing rules to avoid or limit environmental problems caused by undesirable technologies

- information – to help consumers and others to choose less environmentally damaging products

- taxes – to discourage environmentally undesirable consumer choices and industrial practices

- subsidies – to stimulate and support desired developments.

Some of these options might be seen as purely negative, in terms of simply blocking unwanted developments. However, to some extent they can all be seen as positive, because limiting undesirable technologies should stimulate the development of better solutions.

7.3.1 Regulation

In recent years, as noted above, governments in many countries have moved away from intervening directly in the market to setting the boundary conditions in which market interactions occur. This goes well beyond the regulatory policing activities of health, safety and emission control issues.

The emphasis is increasingly on trying to stimulate the development of desired options. For example, in the UK a range of new regulations have been developed covering the life cycle environmental impacts of products, including regulations on recycling and disposal of products and materials, and the establishment of environmental performance criteria for products. These measures are designed to stimulate the development of more environmentally sound products.

7.3.2 Information

market transformation programme

stimulating the market for greener products, for example by providing information to consumers on the environmental performance of products

Governments have also adopted positive measures to stimulate the uptake of new technologies by companies and consumers. For example, the UK government has launched a market transformation programme that aims to change consumer purchasing behaviour by, for example, providing consumers with information about the environmental performance of products. One example is the requirement, initially introduced by the EU, that certain products should have energy labels to indicate their relative energy consumption. Changes in consumer purchasing patterns in response to such schemes should encourage companies to develop more energy efficient products.

7.3.3 Taxes

A direct approach is the use of tax policies to change company behaviours, particularly manufacturing and operational processes – rather than products. For example, in the UK, the imposition of a Climate Change Levy on the energy used by businesses.

From the company's point of view, there are good reasons for corporate change in relation to green technologies. Firstly and most directly, there is growing demand for greener products from consumers. That has been illustrated in previous sections in the case of energy, but it is also apparent in many other sectors. This demand is stimulating competition among companies and new product development.

Secondly, government legislation and new regulations are often powerful stimuli to change corporate policies and new product development strategies. Certainly, in this legislative climate, companies who go green and develop cleaner and greener products and production processes are likely do better commercially than those who do not. This is the win-win argument – both companies and the environment win. But this double win is not an automatic process. There can be losers and some companies may benefit in the short term by avoiding engagement with the new technologies. So governments have a role in setting market conditions that stimulate changes in corporate policies on products.

7.3.4 Subsidies

Perhaps the most direct way in which government can influence technological development is to provide subsidies of some type. In recent years, with the spread of privatisation, large-scale government-funded programmes for major technological projects have become increasingly rare. However, targeted support for the early stages of the innovation process can be a relatively low cost and effective way for governments to steer the innovation process, for example funding interesting new ideas through research and development (R&D) grants.

Another approach, at another stage of the innovation process, is to fund demonstration projects to assist promising but as yet unadopted ideas to come closer to market viability. The dissemination of information to companies about new near-market technologies is an additional option. For example, governments have become increasingly keen to ensure that new ideas emerging in universities and other public bodies are transferred to the private sector. These measures are referred to collectively by the rather ungainly shorthand of RDD&D (research, development, demonstration and dissemination).

The main aim in adopting such approaches is to avoid the gap that often opens up between new ideas and their market uptake. Many potentially viable products seem to need help in making the transition from the pre-competitive or near-market stage to full commercial adoption. Direct financial or technical support for the initial product development – for instance with R&D funding – is a classical example of the technology-push approach to innovation. It can be followed by demonstration and dissemination programmes to help pre-competitive products move nearer to the market. That too can be seen as an extension of technology push, pushing the product further along the innovation process towards the market.

market enablement

a way the government can support the uptake of selected new technologies by adjusting the market context

However, it is also possible to stimulate diffusion by encouraging market pull. For example, a new product's full commercial development and wider adoption can be promoted by priming or modifying the market for an initial period with some form of government regulation or price subsidy. This approach is sometimes known as market enablement, enabling key new technologies to be taken up by the market. Market transformation programmes can also have the same sort of effect, building demand for the product. Some practical examples from the energy field are included in the next section.

Notice that in both approaches the focus is on products and systems that are seen by government as socially and environmentally important, but which may not be easily or rapidly taken up by the market without extra support and effort. To some extent then, governments may have to push companies and consumers that are initially unwilling to change or are at least neutral about the need for change.

Not everyone agrees with government intervention: some believe that market forces ought to dominate and would prefer to leave the direction of innovation and the selection of technology to industry and the market. But even dedicated opponents of intervention accept that governments have to play some role in regulating markets and protecting the environment and consumer interests. Proactive governments can look at the longer-term considerations. As one government minister put it, at the launch of the ESRC Sustainable Technologies Programme in 2002:

> If we are to truly meet the challenges of sustainable development, then the role of Government in the modern world must be to promote innovation in a way that encourages industry to think in terms of long-term sustainability, rather than solely aiming for short-term economic gain.

> (Brian Wilson, UK Department of Trade and Industry)

Obviously there is room for debate over the decisions governments make about which technologies to favour, as well as about the ways in which support is given. That certainly has been the case in terms of renewable energy technologies. The remainder of this section looks at what the UK government has done to promote renewable energy technologies. Similar approaches have been used with other technologies.

7.4 Supporting renewable energy in the UK

As you have read, governments can help to support the initial stage in the innovation process by providing funding for R&D programmes. This is what happened in most industrialised countries following an oil crisis in the mid 1970s when the OPEC oil cartel increased oil prices dramatically. At this time, the USA, UK and many other industrial countries embarked on technology-push programmes to develop renewable energy sources.

However, by the early 1980s the emphasis shifted in most countries to a market-pull approach. This shift was only partly due to the successful emergence of viable technologies from the R&D phase, ready for commercial uptake. In fact many of the technologies still needed R&D support. It was arguably much more a result of a political shift away from government intervention and on to market-led developments, with the emphasis being on achieving competitive success. The underlying approach was well reflected in a response in January 1988 from an Energy Minister to a Parliamentary Question on the role of subsidies and grants. The minister commented, 'The renewable technologies would not be best served in the long term by distorting the market by grant aid or other subsidies for their use' (Michael Spicer, UK Energy Minister).

Nevertheless, in order to achieve its aim of increasing the contribution from renewables, the UK government found it necessary to provide support to enable the newly emerging technologies to enter the marketplace. New technologies usually face a challenge in trying to get established in markets dominated by the existing range of products, and this was clearly a problem for renewables faced with the dominant fossil fuel and nuclear industries. So the government decided to provide extra support to stimulate diffusion, by adjusting the market. As noted earlier, this is sometimes called market enablement – enabling key new technologies to be taken up by the market.

Non-Fossil Fuel Obligation

market-enablement mechanism requiring energy suppliers to obtain some renewable energy and allowing them to pass the cost on to consumers

It did this in a number of ways. Firstly, by introducing a Non-Fossil Fuel Obligation (NFFO), established in 1990. This imposed a small surcharge (initially around 1–2 per cent extra) on electricity consumers' bills, which was used to support renewable energy projects. This was part of a wider fossil-fuel levy scheme, the main aim of which was to provide cross-subsidy support for nuclear power, with the total levy typically adding around 10 per cent to consumers' electricity bills.

With the sell-off of the bulk of the UK's nuclear plants to British Energy, the nuclear element of the scheme was phased out from 1998 onwards, and the proportion of the levy going to renewable energy technologies gradually increased. As a result, by 2000 the NFFO levy scheme led to the installation of around 800 MW of new renewable energy generation capacity.

By this stage some of the technologies were approaching competitiveness with conventional sources and, with a new competitive electricity market system having been introduced, the NFFO scheme was phased out gradually. For new projects, the NFFO was replaced in 2002 by the Renewables Obligation, which you read about in Section 3.

Like the NFFO, the Renewables Obligation aims to stimulate new renewable energy *supply*. In parallel, in 2001 the government imposed a 0.43-pence/kWh surcharge on commercial and industrial *users* of electricity – this is the Climate Change Levy mentioned earlier (Section 3). Companies using renewable energy are exempt from the levy, so this indirect tax acts as a stimulus for the uptake of renewables.

The main aim of these market enablement schemes was to stimulate the development of renewable energy generating capacity and the uptake of the new technologies, through a market-pull approach that compliments the technology-push approach of government R&D funding.

Table 1 indicates the overall allocation of resources to the support measures discussed above.

Table 1   UK support for the renewables

	Research grants[a] (£million)	Renewables Obligation (£million)	NFFO (£million)
1990–91	21.3	–	6.1
1991–92	24.8	–	11.7
1992–93	26.6	–	28.0
1993–94	26.8	–	68.1
1994–95	20.5	–	96.4
1995–96	21.6	–	94.5

	Research grants[a] (£million)	Renewables Obligation (£million)	NFFO (£million)
1996–97	18.5	–	112.8
1997–98	15.9	–	126.5
1998–99	14.4	–	127.0
1999–00	14.9	–	56.4
2000–01	15.9	–	64.9
2001–02	24.0[b]	–	54.7
2002–03	27.6[b]	282.0[b]	unknown
2003–04	29.0[b]	405.0[b]	unknown

[a] Direct government funding for R&D on renewable energy through the DTI's sustainable energy programme and through the research councils via the science budget. Forward projections for RD&D – over £500m allocated for 2002–08 according to the DTI, September 2004.
[b] Estimates.
Source: Hansard, 21 November 2001: Column: 300–01W

7.5   Impacts of the UK support schemes

Apart from the R&D grants, the UK's renewable support schemes shown in Table 1 operate within a competitive market framework, so there are strong incentives to improve the technology and get prices down. That has certainly worked in the case of wind. Whereas in the early rounds of the NFFO schemes in 1991–92, electricity generated by wind projects cost 11 pence/kWh, by 2000 wind projects in some parts of the country were producing electricity at around 2 pence/kWh, competitive with conventional sources. The Renewables Obligation is also based on a competitive market approach. There is a price ceiling, initially set at 3 pence/kWh above the price of conventional power, which means there is competition between generators to undercut this price, and gain contracts from energy retailers.

All of this competition occurs within the requirement set by the government to meet specific annual quotas or targets for renewable energy – for instance 10 per cent by 2010 – which is why the Renewables Obligation is sometimes called a quota scheme. Companies that meet their quotas and accrue surplus Renewables Obligation certificates, can trade them with companies who have a shortfall, which is why the Renewables Obligation is sometimes also called a certificate trading system. You will be looking at the concept of certificate trading later.

The disadvantage of the UK's competition-driven approach is that much less capacity has been installed than in much of the rest of Europe where, in general, a different approach to funding had been adopted, allowing initially higher and guaranteed prices to be charged for new projects. For example, a Renewable Energy Feed in Tariff (REFIT) scheme was adopted in Germany in 1990. New versions of this scheme have been introduced since, including in 2000 the Renewable Energy Law (EEG), but the basic concept has remained the same, to provide guaranteed and favourable prices to get renewables established. For example, wind

REFIT

German tariff scheme where renewable energy generators get guaranteed prices, though prices are reduced in stages as the technology develops projects received up to 9.1 euro cents/kWh (about 6.4 pence/kWh), for the electricity generated, depending on their location. Following a modification in 2000, the price offered to each new participating project was fixed for 5 years, after which time it is reduced to around 6 euro cents/kWh. Subsequently, the electricity prices allowed are progressively reduced (by 1.5 per cent per annum) to take account of operational and technological improvements – a process called degression.

Different levels of support are given for each renewable energy technology, reflecting their state of development. For example PV solar was given much higher initial levels of price support than wind, up to 50 euro cents/kWh at one stage. In 2004, Germany's parliament approved amendments to the renewables legislation, which reduced the overall level of support available for wind generators, while increasing the level of support for biomass. In effect, this reflected the success of the programme for wind, with PV and biomass being expected to follow similar patterns in time.

Not surprisingly, the initial relatively high level of price support led to a boom in construction of wind projects. However, this boom and its subsequent continuation was due not so much to the level of the prices as to the fact that, once agreed for a project, they were guaranteed at known levels by the scheme's formula for a long period ahead, creating a secure climate for investment. In contrast, although some high prices were offered for some projects under the Renewables Obligation – in some cases more than the REFIT scheme offered – they were for short contracts and, given the competitive market, there was no certainty what future prices would be.

The result is that, for example, whereas Germany had installed around 12 000 megawatts of wind capacity by 2003, the UK, which has a much better wind resource, had only installed 550 MW, generating under 1 per cent of UK electricity. By 2006 Germany had installed 18 000 MW of wind capacity, while the UK had reached nearly 1300 MW, including some large offshore projects which benefited from capital grants from the government outside and additional to the Renewables Obligation system.

Table 2 provides some data on the relative cost of renewable energy schemes. This shows that by 2003 the REFIT-type schemes had led to lower overall prices – in some cases much lower. The uncertainty created by market competition within the Renewables Obligation system has meant that prices have not fallen as rapidly as elsewhere, and far fewer projects have gone ahead. In contrast, the guaranteed-price, feed-in-tariff approach adopted in Germany and elsewhere seems to have created a virtuous circle, so that as capacity expands and the market share grows, the subsidy level can be reduced, and costs fall.

The message would seem to be that, so far, reliance on competitive markets has not helped renewables too much in the UK (for more on this, see Butler and Neuhoff, 2004).

Table 2   Cost of wind-generated electricity in 2003

Guaranteed price (feed-in tariff)		Market-based quota	
Country	Cost (euro cents/kWh)	Country	Cost (euro cents/kWh)
Netherlands	9.2	UK	9.6
Germany	6.6–8.8	Italy	13.0
France	8.4		
Portugal	8.1		
Austria	7.8		
Spain	6.4		
Greece	6.4		

Source: Grotz and Fouquet (2005), based on data from German WindEnergy Association (BWE)

However, for its part the UK government argued that it was better to stay with the system that existed rather than to keep changing it. A review by the independent National Audit Office in 2005 did comment that the Renewables Obligation system was expensive, but its consultants claimed the economic 'internal rates of return' on wind projects in the UK were not too dissimilar from those elsewhere (NAO, 2005). That may be true, but that is to be expected given the much higher average wind speeds in the UK and it is indisputable that far less capacity has been installed in the UK than elsewhere.

The difference in the outcomes between the UK and these other countries was not just because the REFIT-type tariff schemes made it easier financially to install more capacity. In addition, the UK's approach seems to have created problems with obtaining planning permissions for the projects. The highly competitive system adopted in the UK meant that wind power developers chose, or you might say had to choose, the more profitable but more environmentally sensitive upland sites, where there were higher wind speeds – typically 7 ms^{-1} was deemed to be needed.

By contrast, the subsidy systems for wind projects in Germany, Denmark and elsewhere meant they could make use of locations with much lower wind speeds – indeed they often had little choice because, for example, Denmark is mostly flat and wind speeds there and in Germany are generally much lower than in the UK. The UK's approach has, it seems, provoked a public backlash against wind, primarily based on visual intrusion, with the result that it has been hard to find sufficient sites for new projects.

Case study   Reactions to wind farms in the UK

National opinion polls indicate overwhelming support for wind energy. For example, a study carried out in 2001 by the British Market Research Bureau for the Royal Society for the Protection of Birds found that only 3 per cent of those asked objected to wind farms. Many subsequent national and regional surveys have found support for wind power running at typically 70–80 per cent. A survey-of-surveys of 42 opinion polls between 1990 and 2002 found that 77 per cent supported wind power, 14 per cent were neutral and 9 per cent against. In a national opinion poll carried out in 2005 for the Institution of Civil Engineers, 77 per cent of those asked supported wind power, though there were significant differences according to the respondents' age: 89 per cent of those aged 16 to 29 and 85 per cent of 30–40-year-olds, compared with 73 per cent of those aged 45–59 and 68 per cent of over-60-year-olds backing wind. Support was weakest in Scotland (65 per cent) and the South West (67 per cent) compared with other areas (86 per cent in Wales, and 84 per cent in East Anglia, the North West and West Midlands).

Obviously care has to be taken with poll data like this. For example, the responses are likely to differ depending on the question asked, and clearly some areas are potentially more sensitive than others. Moreover, responses to hypothetical questions may be different from those to actual projects on your doorstep. During the late 1990s and early 2000s, 60–70 per cent of wind project proposals in the UK were turned down by planning authorities, often after opposition campaigns by local residents.

In response, in order to get the UK wind programme moving ahead more rapidly, the government has put pressure on local councils to set, and meet, their own targets for renewables, within the context of the wider national targets. In 2004 the government introduced new national planning guidelines, with strong guidance to favour wind projects. However, this approach could be seen as provocative and as steamrollering wind projects through, which could increase, rather than reduce, local conflicts.

Given that some of the opposition is based on aesthetic and conservation concerns, the advent of new designs of wind turbine that can operate cost effectively at lower wind speeds may turn out to be more effective as a way of reducing objections, by allowing less invasive siting. In addition, as more people become familiar with wind turbines, opposition to new projects should decrease. That certainly has been the conclusion from the initial projects – once they have been installed local opposition has reduced.

Opposition to poorly sited schemes on environmental grounds – for instance the potential for local problems with bird strikes – might be seen as reasonable and even to be welcomed. Similarly there are wider landscape protection concerns that need to be considered. However, not all the opposition in the UK has been purely on these sorts of grounds. For example, in practice, some of it seems to have been related to fears that local house prices might be affected. There was also sometimes local resentment about the imposition of these projects on communities by large outside companies. At times this could lead to quite strong feeling being aroused. For example, an anti-wind leaflet circulated in Wales in 1994 commented bitterly that Wales was 'in the forefront of being covered in swathes of ugly turbines to line the pockets of foreigners and greedy owners'.

Comparisons with other countries

In this context, it is interesting to look at experience elsewhere with wind projects. As noted in Section 5, in Denmark most of the schemes are owned by local people, often via local co-operatives and farmer and community based enterprises, and there has been much less local opposition. Direct ownership may not be the only factor influencing response to wind projects, but it is interesting that the Danish wind farm enthusiasts often recite the old Danish proverb, 'your own pigs don't smell'. Local objections have also been low in Germany where 45 per cent of the schemes are locally owned, and similarly for the Netherlands, where 40 per cent of the schemes are locally owned. See Table 3.

Table 3 Ownership of onshore wind power in UK, Germany, Denmark and the Netherlands by capacity in 2004

Type of owner	UK (%)	Germany (%)	Denmark (%)	Netherlands (%)
Utilities or companies	98	55	12	60
Farmers	1	35	63	34
Co-operatives	0.4	10	25	6

Source: Toke (2005, p. 20)

There is certainly a striking contrast between the programmes in Germany, Denmark and the Netherlands, which are based to varying degrees on locally owned schemes, and the programme in the UK, which was based almost entirely on schemes developed by large companies (see Table 3). In which case it might be argued that at least part of the remedy is to switch over to local ownership in the UK. The problem with this idea is that the competitive market system established for the UK wind programme makes it hard for small co-operatives or community businesses to succeed. By 2004, only two wind small co-operatives had emerged (Baywind in Cumbria and Cwmni Gwynt Teg in Wales), although some other community-based schemes have been proposed and attempts have been made to increase local support by offering various types of community benefits. This idea will be explored further in Section 10.

It is important that national opinion polls continue to indicate overwhelming support for wind power and more projects are obtaining planning permission. However it seems to be the case that the competitive approach adopted in the UK, based on large companies, initially led to the inappropriate siting of some turbines and created a negative mood that may take some time to dispel.

Clearly then, attempting to enable the market to deliver chosen technologies via competitive mechanisms can create problems. Over-reliance on market forces can sometimes produce backlashes, undermining the original aim. In addition, market enablement of the type just described tends to focus on the near-market options – the technologies that are almost competitive and require interim support to reach commercial success. It tends to leave aside the less developed technologies. In the renewable energy field this means that while wind was picked up by the NFFO, less-developed options, like PV solar and tidal power, were ignored. The Renewables Obligation is, similarly, focused on near-market technologies. REFIT by comparison can be used to support newly emerging options.

Of course, REFIT-type systems have their problems, in terms of loading up utilities with extra costs, some of which are then passed on to consumers. It has been estimated that the extra cost of the REFIT and the subsequent EEG system in Germany was around £1.28 billion in 2003, resulting in an extra charge of around £20 per annum per average consumer, but there seems to have been little concern about this among consumers.

More critically, it could be argued that the guaranteed-price approach might inhibit innovation. Certainly, throwing money at projects is not always a good idea. However, competitive pressures are not absent with REFIT schemes – the incremental reduction in the price as the technology matures is an incentive for continued improvement and development, and regardless of the level of the subsidy, generators who have cost-effective equipment are better placed commercially than those that do not. There has been no lack of technological innovation in the REFIT-type scheme countries such as Germany and, at one stage, Denmark. Both these countries have been at the forefront of wind technology innovation. The same can hardly be said of the UK, which has no significant wind energy manufacturing industry. And, as you have seen, EEG is being used in Germany to support PV solar and biomass.

So a key question is – what sort of support scheme should the UK adopt in future? To put it simply, so far, in the market-driven rush to commercialise near-market technologies, the development of the next batch of new technologies had been downplayed. Clearly, for the longer term, if REFIT is not to be adopted, other types of support are also needed – more technology-push R&D grants for the newly emerging technologies, and market-pull market enablement schemes for the near-market options. For a *continued* programme of successful innovation, there needs to be a smooth transition between the push and pull support mechanism, allowing new technologies to progress through the innovation process and on to deployment.

7.6 Supporting the complete innovation process

Each stage of the technology development process requires different types of financial support, and different diffusion paths apply. In recognition of this, the Non-Fossil Fuel Obligation (NFFO) had separate bands for each technology, with different levels of support being made available. This allowed the level of support for wind to reduce as the technology developed and allowed higher prices to be offered for novel biomass projects, and even for some wave projects. The Renewables Obligation that replaced the NFFO did not retain this feature; instead there is a standard subsidy for all the technologies despite the different level of development and different degrees of markets penetration.

To compensate for this the UK government introduced a system of capital grants for offshore wind and energy crop projects, awarded on a competitive basis, for demonstration projects. Capital grants of £350 million over four years were allocated in the government's 2003 Energy White Paper. Subsequently, the government offered grants for PV solar projects and for new wave and tidal projects via a £50 million marine energy research fund. The government evidently recognised that more grants were needed to ensure successful deployment. In 2005 it announced that the new wave and tidal stream demonstration project would provide grants up to £5 million per project, and an ongoing revenue subsidy (of 10 pence/kWh) for the first five years of operation, this being in addition to the revenue that such projects would obtain from the Renewables Obligation system.

The provision of these grants and extra revenue streams could be seen as an admission that the existing UK support system, with its emphasis on market competition, was not sufficient to ensure the successful full-scale development and deployment of key technologies. It is interesting that the government had to resort to a more traditional direct subsidy approach to smooth the transition between the end of the R&D phase and the beginning of the market enablement phase. Even so, the market emphasis was not ignored: for example, the capital grants for offshore wind projects were awarded based on a competition between rival contractors, and most of the funding for the wave and tidal projects still had to come from the private investment sector, where commercial returns are sought for the investment made.

The main aim of the grants was to stimulate diffusion, particularly the deployment of selected technologies. However, the emphasis was different for each technology. In the case of wave and tidal projects the emphasis was on demonstration of novel ideas, whereas in the case of offshore wind the aim was to support the first few full-scale commercial projects, using relatively untested technology adapted to the new offshore context. Finally, in the case of PV solar, the emphasis was on supporting consumer uptake of well-developed technologies.

In economic terms, the solar support programme might be seen as the most radical in that PV was still expensive, and a long way from market viability. The UK government solar PV scheme, launched in 2002, met half the costs of PV schemes installed in domestic or community buildings. In this case the government was trying to stimulate direct uptake by consumers as a way to prime the market and ensure the technology continues to develop technically and economically. As the Energy Minister put it in a Parliamentary Answer on 26 September 2002: 'Our rationale for supporting photovoltaics is that it is a technology at a relatively early stage of development, but with significant potential for further cost reduction and for meeting our electricity needs in the future.'

There are also other ways in which governments can try to steer, or support, the diffusion process for novel technologies, for example by supporting the growth of new enterprises set up to exploit new technologies. This is not a matter of supporting basic R&D, but rather of seeking to support companies that are trying to bring new ideas to the market. Many such companies are small- and medium-size enterprises (SMEs) and some are new start-up companies, based on developing new product ideas like wave and tidal power, or on new applications of existing renewable technologies. The size of these new companies has been viewed as a positive asset by the government because such companies are seen as innovative, pioneering and competitive.

One strategy to support SMEs was the setting up of innovation centres, some of which have shared technical support facilities. For example, to support work on wave and tidal current energy devices, in 2003 UK government and EU funding was provided for a marine energy test facility on the Orkneys, and a New and Renewable Energy Centre has been established at Blyth in Northumberland.

However, while support for innovation centres is sometimes focused on specific projects like this, in some cases wider, more generic support has been provided to maintain centres that act as nurseries for newly emerging innovation-based companies, working across a range of technologies. Some of these can involve quite small enterprises, indeed in some cases they might involve community-based enterprises that have grown out of the sort of bottom-up initiatives discussed earlier in this block. This point will be looked at further in Section 10.

For the moment, the simple message is that there is a range of ways in which innovation can be stimulated by governments, focusing on various scales and types of organisation, and operating at various points in the innovation process, but each aiming to bring new technologies to the market.

SAQ 7

In terms of the various stages of the innovation process, from invention through to diffusion, how has the focus of the funding provided by the UK government for renewable energy changed from the 1970s onwards?

7.7   Conclusions

This section has reviewed the UK renewable energy programme in order to provide examples of the ways in which the development and deployment of new technologies can be supported. The approaches looked at have ranged from support mechanisms for basic research right through to support for diffusion. However, the emphasis has been on market enablement mechanisms, essentially subsidies to stimulate market uptake.

Clearly, through mechanisms such as the Renewables Obligation, the UK government has tried to prioritise renewable energy. Similar commitments have been made by other countries. Indeed, some other European countries have been offering much more substantial subsidies for renewables. However, a devotee of free market competition might ask why there is a need for subsidies. If there is a need and the technology exists, or can be developed, then the market mechanism will ensure the two come together.

While that may be true in theory, the problem is that it assumes perfect competition on a level playing field, and in reality, given powerful vested interest in the current economic and technological status quo, new entrants usually find it hard to get established. Certainly it can take time. If there are strategic reasons why some new technology needs to be deployed widely and quickly – for example to deal with climate change – then governments may feel the need to intervene to speed up the process.

The problem that then emerges is, how do governments pick the right technologies to push forward? Can the choice of technologies to support be left until they are near to diffusion, or must governments intervene earlier in the innovation process? Must they in effect pick winners before the race has started – and then maintain support throughout the subsequent development and diffusion process? These issues are the topic of the next section.

Key points of Section 7

- Governments may select specific areas of technology for special support to meet strategic objectives such as environmental protection: this support can focus on various stages of the innovation process, ranging from initial R&D through to final diffusion.

- Rather than funding major R&D programmes themselves, many governments these days prefer to adjust and structure the market context to use market forces to deliver desired technological outcomes.

- Diffusion can be assisted by market enablement mechanisms designed to stimulate the rapid and early uptake of selected near-market technologies – the NFFO and Renewables Obligation are examples.

- Market transformation measures such as the provision of information to potential users might also help build a consumer demand.

- For successful innovation new products may need both technology push (perhaps through R&D) and then market pull (perhaps from market enablement).

The key points for Section 7 meet learning outcome 1.5.

8 Picking winners

Picking technological winners is certainly difficult – governments often get it wrong. The history of the development of renewable energy in the UK is littered with examples of false starts, projects abandoned for lack of follow-through, options ignored due to pressures from rival interests, and projects that have been pushed through but subsequently failed. A pessimist might say that governments hardly ever get it right, but equally the market system is not good at looking to the longer term as its focus is on the short term.

This section explores the problems of picking winners at an early stage in the development of renewable energy technology. However, while it identifies problems with this approach when attempted by governments, it also argues that leaving such decisions up to market mechanisms is not a viable way to develop strategically needed technologies. So this section moves from how to pick winners at an early stage to considering ways of supporting the diffusion process.

8.1 Picking a winner

The innovation process is risky; not all new ideas, inventions and designs will successfully pass through the various stages of development and make it to the diffusion process. Given that it is unlikely that sufficient funds will be available to support a wide range of projects, selection must occur at some point. There is inevitably a temptation, for both corporate and governmental interests, to try to pick winners as early as possible in the development process, to avoid wasting money on unnecessary development and ensure successful diffusion.

However, this approach poses problems, not just the risk of getting it wrong and wasting money, but also avoiding the so-called opportunity costs. Inevitably if you focus all your efforts on one technology you ignore others that might have been more successful. There are many examples where initial decisions to ignore or downgrade some option have turned out to be wrong. Box 6 provides some examples from the renewable energy field.

Box 6 Avoiding winners?

Perhaps one of the most celebrated cases of a missed opportunity for picking a winner in the renewable energy field was the UK's initial approach to wind power. In 1973 the UK Department of Energy concluded, in Energy Paper 21, that

> although aero-generators might be considered economic on certain hill sites ... a clear economic case cannot be made for a programme large enough to make a significant contribution to the nation's energy supply.

This type of thinking led to wind power being sidelined in the early phase of the UK's renewable energy programme. Thirty years on, however, wind power had developed elsewhere, and was the fastest growing new energy technology, with by 2005 around 50 000 megawatts of generating capacity installed around the world, but with the UK struggling to catch up by importing wind turbines from Denmark and Germany.

Something similar also happened in the case of wave power. The UK wave energy programme was initiated in the mid 1970s and led to some pioneering designs, some of which were tested as scale prototypes in open water. However, an assessment in 1982 by ACORD, the government's Advisory Committee of Research and Development, concluded that further work on deep-sea wave energy should be halted, based on some high estimates of likely generation costs – estimates of 20 pence/kWh and even 50 pence/kWh were mentioned.

This assessment was strongly challenged at the time. Some critics claimed there was a pro-nuclear bias involved and at the least, the technology had been assessed at too early a stage in its development. The all-party House of Commons Select Committee on Energy commented in 1984 that the suspicion was that wave energy 'was effectively withdrawn before the race began' (Select Committee, 1984, p.xxxii).

The problem of trying to cost a range of novel systems led to disagreement among the experts. Some years later a spokesperson for the Department of Energy told the same Select Committee on Energy that there was 'definitely scope for different judgements at the early stage of the development of a device' (Select Committee, 1992, p.125). Nevertheless, in 1992, a new review of the remaining wave energy projects decided they too should be wound up.

It was not until after a change of government in 1997 that views began to change. Because of funding cutbacks, little new work had been done on wave energy in the UK; however, the political climate had clearly changed. This change was due mainly to growing concerns about climate change. A series of reassessments of wave energy and tidal energy were carried out. This was done initially as part of the UK Technology Foresight programme. The outcome, in March 2001, was an admission by the Department of Trade and Industry that the decision in 1992 to abandon wave energy was wrong:

> The decision was taken in the light of the best independent advice available. With the benefit of hindsight, that decision to end the programme was clearly a mistake.

> (DTI view, quoted in Ross, 2002, p.34)

Wave power has now been resuscitated as an option, and tidal energy is also being pursued with more enthusiasm, and although it is still too early to say whether these new sources will prove as successful as hoped, their combined energy potential is large. The initial decision to downplay these options does seem to have been premature. Certainly that was the view of the House of Commons Select Committee on Science and Technology, which in 2001 commented bitterly that

> given the UK's abundant natural wave and tidal resource, it is extremely regrettable and surprising that the development of wave and tidal energy technologies has received so little support from the Government.

> (Select Committee, 2001, p.iv)

The examples given in Box 6 may seem striking cases of poor decisions, but it is easy to be wise in retrospect. Although there is a need to try to learn from previous mistakes, there is also a need to find a way to balance the risks. With this in mind, and with the fact that the UK has thirty years or so of experience of trying to manage the development of renewable energy technologies, it is interesting to look at what lessons have been learnt on this issue by government.

In its report on non-fossil energy RD&D published in 2003, the Select Committee on Science and Technology commented:

> One cannot find a 'winner' without picking some losers: finding solutions to problems requires the research community to explore all reasonable paths in often unknown and risky territories, and inevitably some will be dead ends or 'dry holes'. Thus risks have to be taken; the right strategy is to pull out once an option has been explored and is a proven 'loser'.

> The [UK] Government has the option of creating a framework of incentives, such as tax credits for RD&D, to devolve the responsibility for picking winners (and inevitably some losers) to industry; but it also has to make choices and take risks too, especially in its support for RD&D where it cannot avoid setting some priorities. The Government has an important role in identifying those of Britain's strengths that are consistent with the industrial environment and the market. It should provide a clear and unambiguous focus.

(Select Committee, 2003)

Inevitably those with favourite projects will want to see them selected for support, and will be frustrated by more cautious approaches. For example, during a House of Commons debate on energy policy in June 2002, a member of parliament, Dr Alan Whitehead, who is a PV solar enthusiast, commented, 'I think we need to start picking winners. I do not think we can afford to stand back and hope that the market alone will make some vital technologies marketable.' The Renewable Power Association, the trade lobby for renewables, put the point like this: 'Spreading R&D funding too thinly fails to achieve results. An element of picking winners is therefore essential.'

The Select Committee on Science and Technology reflected this sense of frustration as follows: 'The Government seems nervous of being accused of picking winners. As a result tough decisions have been avoided. We should be selecting all of those research projects for funding which we have the capacity to execute and which have a reasonable chance of delivering solutions and significant benefit for UK society.'

However, it tempered this enthusiasm for 'letting a hundred flowers bloom' with political realism. 'We appreciate the Government's nervousness about saddling the wrong horse. It would be roundly condemned if it were to put millions into a technology the market would not support. One need look no further than the nuclear industry for instances where this has occurred'. Nevertheless, it added, 'it is reasonable to ask how the Government can have an energy RD&D policy that does not embrace a vision of which technologies should be backed.'

The government's view, however, has typically been much more cautious. For example, during a House of Commons adjournment debate on wave and tidal power in January 2002, the Energy Minister insisted 'We should not be picking winners at this stage. We must let them all flourish to their optimum, and then decide which has the greatest potential for use in the United Kingdom. The market will decide to some extent, but we will have a much more realistic view in a few years' time of which systems can provide significant and economic sources of power.'

The review of UK energy policy conducted in 2001–02 by the Cabinet Office Performance and Innovation Unit (PIU) concluded it was best to avoid foreclosing options. This included the suggestion that the nuclear power option should be kept open. But it also argued that the development of some renewable energy technologies should be supported.

The government White Paper on Energy that emerged in 2003 adopted a similar line. Nuclear power should be kept as an option for the future, in case renewables and energy efficiency did not deliver as much as expected. The paper did not try to select winners from the renewable energy technologies: it left that to the market to decide, within the context set by the Renewables Obligation. However, the government did allocate more funding to some of the less developed options like offshore wave and tidal current power.

SAQ 8

Given that it is difficult to pick winners in terms of identifying areas likely to be worth investing in for innovative effort, why should the government try? Why not leave it up to the private sector and the market to decide?

8.2 Supporting diffusion – not innovation?

The problems of picking winners could be avoided if it was decided to abandon involvement in the early stages of innovation, thereby avoiding the costs and the risks involved with R&D. These costs and uncertainties could be left to other countries to face, with, say, the UK becoming just an informed consumer of any successful or needed technologies developed elsewhere, importing them when they were ready for diffusion. In the case of wind power, the UK seems to have done this already – it has ended up importing machines from Denmark and Germany. The problem with this approach is that the UK then loses out on the advantages of being first in the field with new technologies and on any exports and/or overseas licensing potential. It also has to pay for the imported technology.

The UK has traditionally seen itself as a technological pioneer in many fields, and this has allowed it to develop an industrial base and export and license new technologies around the world. Despite the loss of much of its manufacturing capacity in recent years, the UK has retained a capacity for research and innovation. Indeed, it is usually argued that its knowledge base and innovation potential are major assets in the new world economy. In which case, the country has to continue to invest resources in new ideas. It may be the UK can no longer cover all areas. So perhaps a more subtle response to the question of how to pick winners is that countries should be selective and try to match their investments to areas where they have specific strengths.

The following case study is an assessment of UK options in the renewable energy sector carried out by a UK government-supported agency that set out to look at strengths.

Case study   Selecting energy options for the UK

The Carbon Trust is an independent agency set up by the government to develop business-orientated approaches to reducing carbon emissions. In 2003 it produced a report, *Building Options for UK Renewable Energy*, which reviewed the most cost-effective options for reducing carbon emissions from a commercial 'UK plc' perspective. In other words the report looked at the UK as if it were a commercial enterprise.

First the Carbon Trust listed what it thought were the appropriate levels of support for a technology, 'given its potential to reduce carbon emissions and the potential for UK plc to benefit from its development'. This is the listing:

- If a technology has limited potential to reduce emissions in the UK and has limited scope to create value for UK plc, *do nothing*.

- If a technology has significant potential to reduce emissions in the UK but has limited scope to create value for UK plc because, for example, the value is in the intellectual property behind the technology and this is held overseas, a strategy to *attract inward investment* makes sense.

- If a technology has limited potential to reduce emissions in the UK but has significant scope to create value for UK plc, an *invest-for-export* approach is appropriate. An example would be a small-scale off-grid generation technology, more likely to reach industrial scale in developing countries without a power grid than in a developed economy.

- If a technology has strong potential to both reduce emissions in the UK and create value for UK plc through strong local and export markets, it is appropriate to *invest for domestic use and export*.

With this framework in mind, the report concluded that in relation to onshore wind:

UK plc has a relatively poor competitive position as Danish and German companies have a market share of over 80 per cent in turbine manufacture. However, the UK could still build a significant domestic industry through local component manufacture, installation and operations in onshore wind.

In offshore wind, it said that:

UK plc could develop into a global leader as the industry is at an early stage of development, much of this development is in the UK itself and the UK has design, installation and operations experience in offshore environments.

It added,

Early estimates show that the UK has very significant wave and tidal stream resource, a strong competitive position and, therefore, the potential to become a global leader in the medium term if these technologies can become cost competitive.

Finally it reported that,

The potential for solar PV in the UK is constrained by availability of natural resource, its cost and UK plc's weak competitive position.

Importantly though, the report concluded that,

> Energy efficiency measures to reduce carbon emissions today are cheaper than renewable energy, Government could pursue its environmental goal at lowest cost by focusing on energy efficiency and 'importing' renewable technologies once their cost has been driven down by development at scale elsewhere.

(Carbon Trust, 2003)

Not everyone would necessarily agree with all the details of this analysis, especially because it seems to be mainly concerned with *diffusion* rather than the earlier stages of innovation. For example, technological breakthroughs could change the assessment dramatically, particularly in the PV field; researchers in the UK are working on new polymer PV cells and advanced 'quantum well' PV technology. There is also the thorny and inevitably political question of whether what is good for UK plc is necessarily good for the UK as a whole, or indeed the rest of the world.

There are also methodological issues. For example, focusing just on the reduction of *carbon* emissions may not be the best approach environmentally. Carbon dioxide is certainly the main greenhouse gas, but there are others, and there are other important environmental problems. Focusing solely on carbon emissions takes attention away from issues such as acid gas emissions from fossil-fuelled power stations or the release of radioactive materials from nuclear facilities.

In addition, it is perhaps not wise just to consider each energy option independently. For example, although intermittency is an issue with some renewable energy sources, this problem can be alleviated if power from several different renewables (wind, wave, tidal and solar) is fed into the national grid system – so the variations are balanced out to some extent. It is wiser to think about the role of individual sources and technologies in an integrated sustainable energy system. Nevertheless the Carbon Trust review is a start, and it does highlight the need for a sober assessment of the market and of national capacities.

Exercise 5   Energy efficiency

In the report discussed in the 'Selecting energy options for the UK' case study, in addition to its coverage of renewables, the Carbon Trust noted that *energy efficiency* was by far the most attractive option in terms of the cost per tonne of carbon saved. You have read about some approaches to strategic decision-making in this section of the block, and discussed renewables and energy efficiency in previous sections. With this in mind do you think the Carbon Trust's conclusion that energy efficiency should be given priority is right?

Discussion

It is certainly the case initially that energy efficiency is the cheapest and easiest option, and more attention to energy conservation is obviously vital and urgent. It could therefore be argued that focusing on efficiency would be the best approach, especially because this has been marginalised for so long in favour of supply side investment. However, as has been indicated, there are limits to what energy efficiency can achieve, especially with the continued growth in demand that is likely and the rebound effect.

So it would seem unwise to delay the development of renewables, or rely on others to develop them, simply based on short-term economic assessments. These technologies will get cheaper and the UK could be missing out on export opportunities. Assuming the nuclear option continues to be seen as unviable, the UK is going to need all the renewables that can reasonably be mustered, as well as all the energy savings that can be effectively achieved, in order to reduce carbon emissions by 60 per cent by 2050, as proposed by the government.

It was also mentioned in Section 3 that renewables and energy efficiency can mutually reinforce each other. So it is not a matter of either/or but, arguably, both – assuming there is no reduction in the rate of growth of consumer demand, for instance through lifestyle changes. However, that still leaves the question of the right balance of support for these two options – for example, should it be 50/50, or some other ratio?

Notice that the Carbon Trust, in a subsequent *Renewables Innovation Review* produced in 2004 with the Department of Trade and Industry, suggested that by 2050 renewables could supply 53–67 per cent of UK electricity.

8.3   Following through

After the early phase of innovation and selection of relevant technologies, the next phase is the move from development into diffusion. Trying to ensure a smooth progress through the various stages of the innovation process is not always easy to achieve. There are usually further rounds of choices and selections to be made. For example, within each area of technology a flurry of competing ideas often emerges with a range of rival organisations becoming involved, and it usually takes time for a potential winner to emerge from the development process. Figure 21 provides a schematic description of the development pattern for new technologies like renewables, illustrating how they move through stages, and looking at the number of companies and the number of projects that are typically involved at each stage.

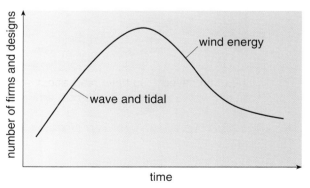

Figure 21   Development of renewable technologies leading to fewer firms and designs as a market matures – with wind-driven generators moving toward maturity ahead of wave-driven and tide-driven generators

Initially the situation is relatively open ended and fluid, with a few competing ideas and pre-commercial designs emerging from a few innovative companies. Then more companies become involved and more designs emerge, leading to a transitional consolidation phase, as the technology moves to be near-market; that is, towards commercial acceptance. As this process continues there is usually a degree of industrial concentration; some of the smaller companies fall by the wayside and others are absorbed into larger companies, although occasionally a small pioneering company becomes the new large dominant company. So, one way or another, this stage usually leads to a period of rationalisation when a few companies become dominant, focusing on a few specific, mature, designs taken fully into the market.

This pattern can be seen in most industrial sectors – an early flurry of ideas from an increasing number of companies, followed by the emergence of a few dominant companies and a consolidated range of technologies and designs. In the renewable energy sector, in the 1980s and 1990s there was a sudden flush of designs for wind turbines of different types, and by the early 2000s wind power had become a mature technology, focused on the basic three-blade propeller design, with a limited number of companies having established dominance.

In contrast, in the early 2000s, wave and tidal generators were still at an early stage of technological development, with many small companies still being at the project demonstration stage with a range of designs. Tidal current technology was, for example, in its infancy and a range of prototypes of different designs were being tested at sea. Figure 22 shows two different tidal current energy collection concepts that emerged in the UK. Several other novel designs have also emerged from the UK and elsewhere and it remains to be seen which design will prove to be best. PV solar is a little harder to fit into the pattern.

(a)   (b)

Figure 22   (a) Stingray tide-driven hydroplane developed by The Engineering Business and tested on the seabed off the Shetlands in 2002 and 2003. The tidal flow makes the hydrofoils oscillate up and down. (b) Seaflow 300 kW tide-driven prototype on test off the coast of north Devon in 2003. It is like an underwater wind turbine, with a conventional propeller mounted on a pile driven into the seabed. The propeller can be raised out of the water (as shown) for maintenance. Sources: (a) The Engineering Business Ltd; (b) Marine Current Turbines[TM] Ltd

By the early 2000s the technology was well developed with a few large companies dominating the field but it has not yet been widely diffused in the UK and it is still open to major technological advances to improve the technology or process innovations to reduce the cost of manufacture.

It is relatively easy to identify development patterns like those illustrated in Figure 21 once they have occurred – that is, in retrospect. However, once the initial general pattern has been established it may be possible to use curves like this to forecast likely subsequent developments. This is valuable because it may help decide whether to continue supporting specific lines of development. As you will now see, this type of approach can be strengthened by the use of learning curve analysis.

8.4 Learning curves

Inevitably some technologies turn out to be unsuccessful commercially. Perhaps more worryingly, some may be dumped before they have had a chance to prove themselves because it takes time to move from experimental prototypes to commercial-scale operation and investors may lose confidence if rapid progress is not made. However, there is an analytical technique that can sometimes help indicate likely trends in economic development and which may therefore ensure successful follow-through rather than premature abandonment of projects. This is known as learning curve assessment.

learning curve

performance of a new technology plotted against market uptake, showing the rate of development as experience is gained and as markets expand

There is usually a process of gradual improvement in technical performance and reduction in costs as the technology develops, experience is gained and markets are established. This trend will usually be pronounced during the early stages of the product's development, but it will also continue when and if volume production and wider diffusion starts. At that point, economies of production volumes and scale begin to apply – it is cheaper to produce more things of the same kind – and experience with increasing numbers of the product in a widening and increasingly competitive market leads to further improvements in costs and performance.

This trend is familiar enough when you think about, for example, the way the price of consumer electronics falls. Video cassette recorders, CD players, DVD players, and so on typically started out costing thousands of pounds, but soon dropped to hundreds as the market built and volume production got under way, with competition from rivals providing a key impetus.

Figure 23(a) provides an example based on the price of electricity produced from wind turbines in Denmark, which was the initial leader in this field. As can be seen, as the technology was first developed there was an initial rapid fall in price per kilowatt-hour of electricity generated, and then, as the technology moved to wider use in Denmark and worldwide, there was a slightly lower rate of price reduction, with economies of production scale and market scale beginning to play a role.

Figure 23(b) shows the scale of the uptake in terms of the gradually increasing growth of the total generating capacity (kilowatts) in use worldwide up to 2000 – the majority of the machines at this stage still being Danish. To some extent the growth in use will have been a result of the reduction in cost, but it is a two-way interaction – expansion of production or use also leads to reduced costs and increased performance.

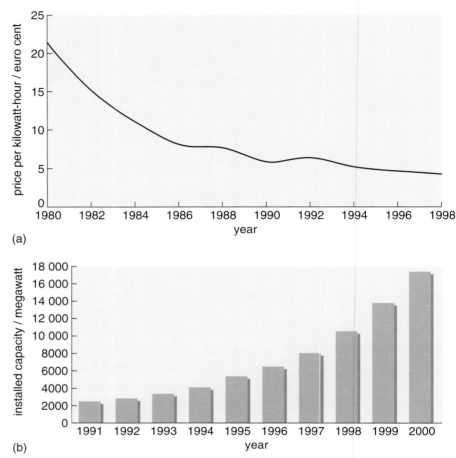

(a)

(b)

Figure 23 **(a) Price of electricity from wind turbines in Denmark, 1980–1998. (b) Growth of world wind turbine generator capacity, 1991–2000.**
Source: Gross, Leach and Bauen, 2002

The implication of this analysis is that it can be worth taking a longer-term view of new technologies and their funding. 'Staying the course', rather than expecting rapid results, may be the best strategy.

Obviously not all technologies will successfully navigate through the learning and development process and go on into the diffusion phase, but studies over a wide range of technologies have indicated that the pattern of improvement is usually similar, regardless of the specifics of the technology. This can be demonstrated by plotting technical performance – often measured in terms of price or cost – on a graph against the volume of product sold or in use, using logarithmic scales for both axes (Figure 24). In effect, this is combining the curves like those in Figure 23(a) and Figure 23(b) into one plot, showing the rate of progress in terms of cost related to volume sold or in use. For most technologies, on this type of log-log graph, a straight line results.

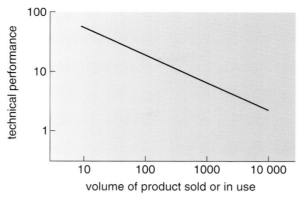

Figure 24   Learning curve on a log-log plot

This is quite a striking result – especially because it seems to be independent of which technology is involved. This straight line usually continues across the development and subsequent commercial diffusion period. Of course, at some point in the product's history, the potential for learning will be exhausted and the line will flatten out – it never reaches zero cost – so the pattern cannot be extrapolated indefinitely. Also, in some cases there may be rapid learning at the early prototype stage. In general, however, for most technologies and for most of their development and diffusion periods, the straight-line relationship holds.

However, there are differences in the slope of the line, depending on the technology involved. The slope for most technologies has been found to be in the range 15–30 per cent. Notice that, as with road gradients, the higher the percentage, the steeper the slope and the faster the progress towards higher performance or lower cost.

Although these log-log graphs usually show straight lines, not curves, they tend to still be referred to as learning curves. In essence what they provide is an indication of how sensitive the price-cost of the technology is to the scale of production. As has already been said, these lines cannot be extrapolated into the long-term future. But because the straight lines seem to hold over a wide range of technologies and over most technologies' development and diffusion periods, learning curves offer a way to identify likely future costs of new technologies, at least in the medium term. This approach is an improvement on engineering assessments of eventual likely costs, which usually rely on the assessment of costs based on early prototypes.

SAQ 9

What do you think is the explanation for the linear nature of log-log learning curves? Why does a straight line emerge covering *all* the various stages of innovation?

8.5   Lessons of learning curves

Learning curve analysis can have significant implications for policy-makers. For example in the case of photovoltaics (PV), when prices were still high, the learning curve slope for solar was found to be around 18–20 per cent by the UK Cabinet Office's Performance and Innovation Unit in its 2001 study of renewables (PIU, 2001a) (Figure 25). This suggests the market enablement programme that Germany had

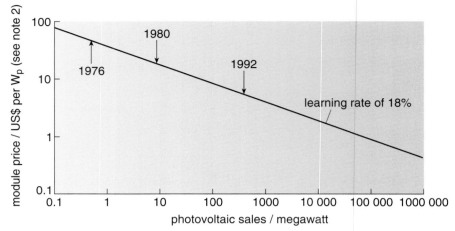

Note 2: W_p is the theoretical peak power output
in watts of a photovoltaic module

Figure 25   Learning curve for solar photovoltaic modules on the global market

initiated for solar PV, with initially high prices being condoned and met with generous subsidies, was a reasonable approach – the scheme was for 100 000 installations supported by the REFIT system.

Following this study, the UK, which had up to that point more or less sidelined PV, subsequently tried to catch up with its own subsidised PV market deployment and innovation support programmes, although they were on a much smaller scale than in Germany. The view in the UK still seemed to be that PV was a longer term option, an assessment reinforced by the DTI's Renewable Innovation Review, published in 2004, which concluded that solar PV would not be competitive by 2020 unless there were 'very substantial reductions in costs', which were likely to require a 'breakthrough to next generation technology'. This could be a self-fulfilling prophecy if insufficient market support is made available.

Figure 26 shows a range of learning curves for various energy technologies, plotting costs of energy generation against cumulative energy generated. As can be seen, wind and PV both have steep learning curves. But PV, which starts from a high price, has a steeper slope than wind – with much less capacity installed so far. What this indicates is that PV prices fall more rapidly as production volumes increase than is the case for wind turbines. This is a strong argument for market enablement for PV, because it appears that although wind power has already passed down its learning curve to low prices, PV might in future achieve price reductions even faster than the wind power did.

Figure 26 also suggests that both wind and PV should, or at least could, do better than some of the other energy technologies. For example, gas-fired combined-cycle turbines that are widely used, exhibited little development in terms of cost reduction over the period shown; the learning curve for this technology is flat. A similar curve can be seen for supercritical (high temperature steam) coal combustion. But by contrast a newer entrant, biomass combustion, is beginning to make progress down its quite steep learning curve.

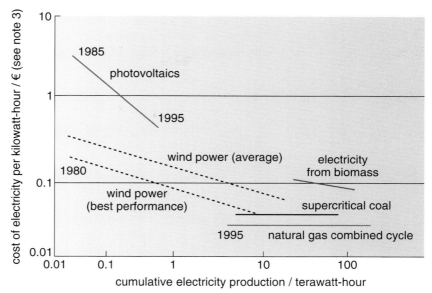

Note 3: unit for price was originally given as European Currency Unit (ECU), which corresponds with the euro

Figure 26 Learning curves for some electricity generation technologies
Source: IEA (2000)

It is perhaps worth mentioning that the Cabinet Office Performance and Innovation Unit study mentioned above found that, by contrast, the slope for nuclear reactor technology was only around 5.8 per cent – which they attributed to the fact that it was a 'mature' technology involving large, inflexible projects with long lead times. They also argued the frequent emergence of completely new designs meant there was less technological continuity, less opportunity for economies of production scale, and less opportunity for learning. Of course, completely new nuclear technologies may emerge and start on a new learning curve, but this analysis led the Cabinet Office team to view the further development of nuclear power as at best a longer term option (PIU, 2001b). In the main, it saw renewables as more likely to prosper, if given proper support.

The simple message from learning curve analysis is that for new technologies with reasonable initial learning curve projections, the rate of improvement can be maintained by support for early exposure to real world use and application in the diffusion phase. That is when modifications come thick and fast and when economies of production scale can be obtained. But one thing is clear – without sufficient support to move the technology on, and to build a market for it, you are unlikely get much improvement. Expecting rapid results is foolish, as is only looking for technologies with initial low costs. A longer-term perspective is required, as well as support for market creation.

8.6 Conclusion

What you have looked at in this section are the problems of picking winners and the case for taking a longer term approach to the selection and development of new technologies. Based on the lessons from learning curves, it is argued that seeing it through to market uptake may help technologies to develop and become fully economically viable. Clearly these lessons are relevant to government, especially given its strategic environmental concerns, but they are also relevant to industry, which after all needs to innovate successfully to prosper.

Key points of Section 8

- Selecting the right technologies – picking winners – is difficult, so some governments (and companies) may decide to opt out of new technology development and wait for the market to pick up successful technologies developed elsewhere.

- Leaving technology selection up to the short-term perspective typical of markets can mean that options that may turn out to be important in the longer term are not supported: learning curve analysis suggests a longer-term view may be wiser.

- The problems of adopting a short-term approach, focusing on a rapid move to commercial competitiveness, seem to be exemplified by the UK's approach to renewable energy technology.

The key points for Section 8 meet learning outcomes 1.5, 1.6, and 1.7.

9 Global diffusion

The previous two sections have focused mainly on the situation in the UK. However, in the same way that climate change is a global phenomenon, the development and diffusion of renewable energy is also a global phenomenon. In this section you will look briefly at the global situation, to identify different approaches that have been adopted to the development and diffusion of renewable energy technologies around the world.

9.1 Emissions trading

Many countries have their own national support schemes providing grant aid and other subsidies – for example the REFIT system. At the same time, however, attempts have been made to try to stimulate the uptake of renewables and other sustainable energy technologies globally via the development of emissions trading systems.

The international agreement on climate change policies negotiated at Kyoto in Japan in 1997 included targets for reducing greenhouse gas emissions by around an average of 5 per cent globally, with the UK being required to reduce its emissions by 12.5 per cent during the commitment period 2008–12. The Kyoto arrangements also included proposals for helping to achieve these targets, via a global market-based system in which tradable emissions certificates or credits are issued by governments to companies who reduce emissions. These credits are set against national targets, which are derived from the overall targets set by the Kyoto agreement.

Within this type of system, if a company can get more carbon credits than it needs, by reducing its emissions below the target, it can sell them to a company that can't meet its target. There is therefore an incentive for companies to earn more credits – or at least to avoid having to buy them. This creates a secondary market for credits issued by government agencies – a market for certificates or credits separate from the actual sale of electricity. This reflects companies' success at meeting the government-imposed targets for renewable energy production, or more generally, for emission reductions.

Renewables Obligation certificates

tradable certificates issued to energy supply companies for each megawatt-hour of renewable energy they have purchased under the Renewables Obligation

The UK's Renewables Obligation system in fact involves a version of this approach. Under this system companies are awarded Renewables Obligation certificates (ROCs) based on the number of megawatt-hours of green electricity they have purchased. If an energy supply company has been able to earn more of these ROCs than they need to meet the target set for that year, they can trade the excess with companies that do not have enough. So the ROCs become a valuable 'virtual' commodity, with the ROC market creating an incentive for all concerned to increase the amount of renewable energy used, either to earn more ROCs to sell, or to avoid having to buy them.

During the first year of operation, ROCs were changing hands at the equivalent of over 5 pence per kilowatt-hour, about 3 pence/kWh more than the average wholesale price of electricity. This price level was the result of a government decision to make it possible for energy supply companies who did not have sufficient ROCs to meet their annual target, to buy themselves out of the scheme, by paying a 3 pence/kWh fine. This 'buy out' price sets the overall price which supply companies are willing to pay for green power or ROCs. It also puts a ceiling on the extra cost of complying with the Renewables Obligation – a cost the companies are allowed to pass on to consumers. The government's aim was to try to keep the extra costs to consumers to around 4–5 per cent by 2010.

Similar green certificate trading schemes have been developed in some other EU countries, and in principle the various permits could be traded internationally, although that has proved difficult in practice, given their value is dependent on the local – that is, national – context for green power generation. However, the EU has developed an emissions-trading scheme (EU-ETS), which came into operation in 2005 and covers the whole EU. Rather than focusing on certificates for power generation from green sources, it focuses on the tonnes of emissions avoided by using renewables, or avoided in other ways. This scheme is based on imposing an overall cap or limit on emissions of greenhouse gases from power stations and other industrial plants. In the initial phase (2005–07) the cap focuses just on carbon dioxide emissions but may be widened to other greenhouse gases later.

Companies that cannot meet the emissions requirement are fined €40/tonne of carbon, but those able to get their emissions below the cap can sell their excess carbon credits. So a market in credits is created, and a process of carbon trading is established. By 2005 EU-ETS carbon credits were being traded for €30/tonne C.

carbon trading

trading of certificates given to companies that have reduced carbon dioxide emissions; because the certificates have a value they can be traded

In parallel, an international carbon trading system is being considered, so the EU emissions trading system could ultimately become part of a global carbon trading system, as envisioned in the Kyoto protocol. Certainly, the UK government, along with most of the rest of the EU, has indicated that it sees carbon-trading schemes like this as being one of the main ways in which the take-up of renewable energy technologies will be promoted in the future.

Of course this cap-and-trade approach relies on the existence of an agreed and binding cap and on careful monitoring and accreditation of claimed emissions reductions, which implies significant bureaucratic involvement. This approach also imposes extra costs on the companies involved, which is usually passed on to consumers, although this cost should be less than with direct subsidy schemes. In seeking to meet the targets and earn emissions credits, the supply companies are also likely to focus on the most economic and well established of the green energy technologies. So the trading system approach is not suitable for the support of newer, less developed, renewable energy options; as you have seen, these options may need other forms of support, like the capital grant scheme in the UK for offshore wind and PV solar.

One attraction of the REFIT-type guaranteed-price system used in Germany and elsewhere is that such schemes can be flexible enough to cover emerging technologies needing significant subsidies as well as technologies that are maturing. Concerns about the loss of flexibility have led to some resistance to emissions trading schemes in countries where REFIT-type subsidy schemes have been operating. To some extent this is a matter of timing. For example, arguably, in some locations, on-land wind power should no longer need significant extra support over and above what an emissions trading system will provide. When this block was first written in 2005, it had been agreed within the EU that both approaches can continue in parallel, at least for a period. However, in the longer term, REFIT-type subsidies will no doubt be phased out as the existing technologies mature and trading approaches are likely to take over, but there will still be a need to find ways to support the next wave of new technologies.

Despite their shortcomings, the longer-term benefits of emissions trading systems are clear. These systems offer an increasing incentive for companies and countries to reduce emissions, not just to avoid fines, but also so they can become involved with what could be an increasingly lucrative carbon-trading market. Market forces have therefore been enlisted to support an environmental aim – emission reduction – and should help to stimulate the adoption of renewables and other low or zero carbon technologies, at least within countries where emission caps are in operation. You will be looking at the situation elsewhere in the world later. For the moment I'll look at the EU and explore the level of renewable energy uptake that different support schemes have achieved.

9.2　Market take-up in the European Union

The European Union has developed a Directive on Renewable Energy that specifies targets for each member country to aim for by 2010 (Table 4). This builds on the levels of contribution each has achieved so far, and the prospects for the future. Table 5 indicates the level reached by 2001. It is hoped that along with the various national support systems the EU emissions trading system, which started operating in 2005, will help to ensure the 2010 targets are met.

As can be seen, the UK has a relatively poor position in these league tables and its target for 2010 is lower than most, including those for some of the countries who joined the EU in 2004 (Table 6). To be fair, one reason why countries like Sweden, Finland and Austria do so well in these league tables is because, unlike the UK, they have extensive and widely used biomass (forestry) resources, used mainly for heating, and large hydro electricity resources. However, even looking just at electricity – therefore excluding at least some of the biomass – the UK still does not fare much better. Moreover, the situation does not improve much for the UK even when hydro is also excluded (Table 4, right-hand column).

The international comparisons also highlight some other interesting differences between the countries. For example, apart from Luxembourg, the countries at the bottom of Table 4, France, Belgium and the UK, have all invested heavily in nuclear power in the past, and Belgium and France have only recently started seriously supporting renewables.

Table 4   EU Directive 2010 targets for electricity from renewables, ranked in order of excluding large hydro (third column)

EU country	Including large hydro (%)	Excluding large hydro (%)
Denmark	29.0	29.0
Finland	35.0	21.7
Portugal	45.6	21.5
Austria	78.1	21.1
Spain	29.4	17.5
Sweden	60.0	15.7
Italy	25.0	14.9
Greece	20.1	14.5
Netherlands	12.0	12.0
Ireland	13.2	11.7
Germany	12.5	10.3
UK	10.0	9.3
France	21.0	8.9
Belgium	6.0	5.8
Luxembourg	5.7	5.7
EU 15	22.1	12.5

Table 5   Renewable energy as a percentage of total primary energy in 2001

EU country	Percentage
Sweden	29.4
Finland	22.4
Austria	21.5
Portugal	13.7
Denmark	10.4
France	7.0
Spain	6.5
Italy	5.6
Greece	4.6
Germany	2.6
Ireland	1.7
Luxembourg	1.6
Netherlands	1.4
United Kingdom	1.1
Belgium	1.0

Source: International Energy Agency, quoted in *Hansard* (15 October 2003)

Table 6 EU accession-country renewable electricity production in 1999 and targets for 2010

Country	1999/(%)	2010/(%)
Cyprus	0.05	6.0
Czech Republic	3.8	8.0
Estonia	0.2	5.1
Hungary	0.7	3.6
Latvia	42.4	49.3
Lithuania	3.3	7.0
Malta	0.0	5.0
Poland	1.6	7.5
Slovakia	17.9	31.0
Slovenia	29.9	33.6
average	5.4	11.1
EU 25 (target reduced from the EU 15 target)		21.0

Source: EC/Platts Renewable Energy Report I (2003)

The UK, which in 2005 obtained around 21 per cent of its electricity from nuclear plants, still allocates around half of its R&D budget for energy developments to nuclear technology even though there is no commitment at present to building new plants – some of the research is on clean-up and safety. There have been moves to consider replacing the UK's elderly nuclear plants with new nuclear plants as and when the former are retired – a review of the options started in early 2006 – but one argument against that has been that this could divert money from the renewable energy programme.

Belgium gets about 57 per cent of its electricity from nuclear plants, but has decided to phase them out and is pushing ahead with renewables. France obtains around 75 per cent of its electricity from nuclear plants, but following the election of a socialist government with green tinges in 1997, the Superphoenix fast breeder reactor programme was abandoned and an interim moratorium on new nuclear plants was imposed, pending a reassessment of energy policy. Although it was subsequently decided to keep the nuclear option open, with one new plant planned, France has also launched an ambitious renewables programme, with a target of 10 000 megawatts for wind by 2010. Interestingly, France has adopted a REFIT-type support tariff system for this programme – it evidently wants to catch up rapidly.

This same pattern seems to hold for most other countries. The renewable energy leaders are non-nuclear, or are phasing out nuclear. Following a major public debate in the 1970s Denmark took a decision not to use nuclear power. In 1999, Germany, following the election of a socialist–green government, decided to close its 19 nuclear plants – the first one shut in 2004 – and has committed itself heavily to renewables. Spain is becoming one of the EU leaders in wind and PV solar, and the socialist government elected in Spain in 2004 pledged to phase out nuclear power. In contrast, Finland has decided to build a new nuclear plant, and this commitment seems to have led to a reduced emphasis on developing its large renewable energy resource (WISE, 2004, p.7).

Several of the ex-Soviet states who joined the EU in 2004 had major nuclear programmes, but some are now phasing them out, in some cases as a requirement of EU accession, and most are opting for renewables. For example, under the terms of its EU entry agreement, Lithuania is phasing out nuclear power – which used to provide 80 per cent of its power using Chernobyl-type RBMK technology – and is beginning to develop biomass and wind in particular. Slovakia, similarly, is backing away from its Soviet nuclear legacy. As Table 6 shows, it aims to significantly expand its already large renewables contribution.

As already noted, another general point that emerges from international comparisons is that the renewable leaders have all used, or are using, REFIT-type support systems, notably Denmark, Germany and Spain. France has also now adopted a REFIT-type scheme, as has Ireland. In addition, some of the new EU members have adopted REFIT-styled approaches. As Table 6 shows, Latvia, which is non-nuclear, currently gets a large contribution from renewables, which it is planning to expand using a REFIT-style support system. Non-nuclear Estonia has also adopted a REFIT-type approach in its effort to develop its renewable energy resources rapidly, by a factor of 25 by 2010.

In 2005, 18 of the EU's 25 countries were using REFIT-type schemes. The UK, Sweden, Italy and Poland had competitive quota trading-type schemes of various types, while Denmark, which initially used REFIT, was in the process of setting up a quota-trading-type scheme. Slovakia and Lithuania use other types of support (Bechberger and Reiche, 2005).

Whichever support system is used the EU clearly sees rapid deployment of renewables as a priority and most member countries agree.

Quite apart from the need to meet international environmental obligations on emissions, there are clearly strategic commercial advantages in being the first to develop a technology on a significant scale, as Denmark and then Germany found in relation to wind turbines. Rodney Chase, deputy group chief executive officer and chief executive of BP Oil, has commented,

> It could well be that the first country to seriously address the issues of creating a market for renewables would become the central location for a major new international business sector, with all the positive consequences that carries in terms of economic activity and employment.

(Chase, 1998)

You will be looking at the situation outside Europe below but clearly there could be a growing market for renewable energy technology around the world – estimates by the World Energy Council range up to £1400 billion per annum globally by 2020 – and there are advantages in being first to get into it.

SAQ 10

In the 'Selecting energy options for the UK' case study in Section 8, the Carbon Trust outlined the conditions under which it might be worth the UK getting into renewables. How does its analysis compare with the views of Chase, as quoted above?

9.3   Outside the Kyoto zone

The Kyoto protocol's targets only apply formally and legally to the industrialised countries who are party to the agreement, which means they are not binding on the USA or Australia. Australia was actually given a dispensation to increase its emissions by 10 per cent under the draft Kyoto rules, partly because it is heavily involved with exporting coal to Asia, but it still felt unable to sign up formally. Perhaps surprisingly, given its climate, it only has a moderate renewable energy programme, with a target of obtaining 2 per cent of its electricity from renewables by 2010 – compared with 10 per cent in the UK.

Under the draft Kyoto agreement, the USA was required to reduce its emissions by 7 per cent but it was unwilling to sign up to this. Instead it has adopted a different approach. Although some states and some cities have initiated their own schemes, there are no national carbon targets or trading arrangements. Instead, in the early 2000s, the federal government launched a clean-energy technology development programme, including a $1 billion Future Gen project to convert coal into gas and store carbon emissions, and a $1.7 billion hydrogen car project aimed at eliminating carbon dioxide emissions from cars. Much of the emphasis seems to be on finding ways to continue to use fossil fuels, coal in particular, but there are also programmes to support renewables, and perhaps more contentiously, nuclear power.

The US government has claimed that technology-led programmes like this will achieve emissions reductions more effectively than regulatory measures, and in particular will do so without undermining the US economy. In this context, it is interesting that in 2005 the USA, Australia, India, China, South Korea and Japan signed an Asian–Pacific climate change and clean technology pact aimed at developing and deploying new clean energy technologies including renewables, carbon capture for fossil-fuel plants, and nuclear power plants. However, unlike the Kyoto arrangements, there were no mandatory carbon emission reduction targets set, nor any provisions for carbon trading.

This is not the place for an extended analysis of this technology-led approach, nor its potential for success. However, it has to be said that the USA's greenhouse gas emissions are the largest in the world, around 36 per cent of the world total, and they have continued to rise, with carbon dioxide emissions rising by 16 per cent between 1990 and 2004. This is hardly surprising given that, in terms of the percentage of total energy generation, the USA is still relatively low down the renewable energy league for the industrialised world. In contrast most signatories to the Kyoto protocol have been making reductions in line with the Kyoto targets (Table 7).

Table 7   Electricity from renewable energy as percentage of electricity supplied in 2002 (selected countries)

	Proportion of total electricity supplied, including large hydro (%)	Proportion of total electricity supplied, not including large hydro (%)
Austria	8.9	1.2
Denmark	18.3	18.1
Finland	28.1	13.7
Germany	7.2	3.8
France	13.2	1.0
Italy	18.1	3.1
Japan	13.1	2.7
Spain	14.9	5.5
UK	2.9	1.5
USA	8.8	2.2

Sources: adapted from International Energy Agency and US Department of Energy

Nevertheless, by virtue of its size, wealth and technological prowess, in terms of absolute amounts the USA currently generates more energy from renewables – both 'new' renewables and large hydro – than any other country, and it is clearly a major player in the innovation field. In time its technology programmes could have a major impact on world developments. Even so, it is interesting in policy terms that the USA, and it seems the new Asian–Pacific pact, has returned to a technology-push approach, rather than one based on using regulation to engage market mechanisms, as in the EU.

One of the USA's objections to the Kyoto protocol was that the emissions rules applied only to the industrialised nations. Countries in the developing world, including, crucially, China and India, were expected to join in on a voluntary basis. Subsequent to the Kyoto agreement there have been international negotiations on what will happen after the current Kyoto agreement runs out in 2012. It seems likely that attempts will be made to include countries like China and India, who are industrialising rapidly, in the formal emissions cap system, although there are some fears that the new Asian–Pacific pact may undermine that process.

clean development mechanism

carbon-trading agreement designed to reward industrial countries that invest in carbon dioxide emission-reducing projects in developing countries

Meanwhile, a version of the carbon trading concept was proposed in the Kyoto agreement to try to ensure there would be a commercial incentive to seek emission reductions in developing countries; this is known as the clean development mechanism (CDM). Under the CDM, low carbon projects initiated by developed countries in developing countries can earn carbon credits. Projects might include renewable energy schemes, improvements in energy efficiency and some types of forestry. The first CDM project was agreed in 2004 and involved methane gas collection from a landfill site in Brazil, initiated by the Netherlands.

As can be seen, carbon or emissions trading systems try to use market forces to reward companies who use low-carbon technologies. Not everyone is happy with the resultant virtual market, based on trading permits and certificates, which may not be directly linked to actual emissions. Reliable verification of the real-world delivery of emissions reductions is obviously a key requirement. But the scale of carbon trading could be large. Even before the Kyoto protocol was formally ratified, speculative ad hoc trading got under way, with more than 65 trades totalling between 50 million and 70 million tonnes in the period 1997–2002, with prices ranging up to £10 per tonne of carbon. It seems likely, then, that international carbon trading could become a major driver for the diffusion of new green energy technologies.

9.4   Technology transfer

As well as stimulating the use of green energy technologies in the developed world, the growth of carbon trading and the clean development mechanism could, with the support of companies in the developed world, stimulate the diffusion of new energy technologies in the developing world. This technology transfer between industrialised and developing countries is often seen as a key solution for supporting economic development in less developed countries.

technology transfer

transfer of technologies and expertise from industrialised countries to developing countries; sometimes used for the transfer of other knowledge

Notice the term technology transfer is a general one. It can apply to the transfer or dissemination of technological knowledge, skills or experience in a variety of situations. The term can be applied to the transfer of knowledge between universities and industry within a country. Indeed, over the past few decades governments have been increasingly keen to support transfer of this sort and there has been a growth of science parks located near universities, in an attempt to build links between academia and industry and create high-tech spin-off enterprises. However, in this discussion I am focusing on international technology transfer between industrial and developing countries.

Technology transfer is not as simple as might initially be expected. There are problems with deciding which technologies should be transferred and how such decisions should be made and acted on. For example, environmental campaigners have fought to ensure the clean development mechanism is not used to support the transfer of nuclear technology and there have been strong pressures to resist the inclusion of large hydro projects, which resulted in their exclusion from the CDM. The argument against these technologies is based not only on their environmental impact, but also on the premise that if large projects like this were allowed to get support from the CDM, that would crowd out smaller-scale renewable energy projects that are more suitable for local economic development (Figure 27).

Even when it comes to smaller scale projects, there can be problems with selecting appropriate technologies, especially if the transfer is a simple one-way top-down process, where new products are 'parachuted' in. The technology may not be suited to local conditions, and there may not be the necessary technical and skill infrastructure for successful long-term operation and maintenance.

Perhaps more importantly, parachuting in already-developed technology will not help create the capacity for indigenous technological innovation, which is needed if the local economy is to prosper. It may be that local involvement with the development of products tailored to local conditions could help produce more appropriate products, better suited to local needs and conditions, and

Figure 27   Photovoltaic panels in an application in the developing world
Around 2 billion people in developing countries do not have access to mains electricity

help build the capacity for economic and technological development. One example is the wind-powered water pumping system developed in the UK by the Intermediate Technology Development Group, which is designed for local manufacture, and allows adaptations to be made to suit local conditions.

Just as with the examples in the developed world of wind turbines and solar collectors discussed earlier, the involvement of users and consumers in the developing world is seen as crucial for successful diffusion. There is no shortage of examples of failures of the top-down approach. One was an attempt in the 1970s to promote the use of solar cooking devices, designed in the West, in rural areas of countries like India. The cookers used parabolic reflectors to focus heat, and could, it was hoped, replace the use of firewood, which was becoming scarce, or dung, which was a valuable organic material. Sadly, it was not appreciated that in many developing countries cooking is not done until after sundown, when people come in from their work in fields.

Simple practical incompatibilities like this should be easy to avoid, but there could be much more to be gained by local involvement. Indeed, following a more carefully targeted programme of deployment, solar cookers have subsequently found niche markets, for example in South Africa.

A more recent example of the need to consider local requirements is the idea promoted by some environmental groups and aid agencies that the early, widespread and rapid adoption of solar PV should be encouraged as an aid to development. Around 2 million people in the developing world do not have access to grid electricity, so deploying PV solar at the village level seems a good solution. Certainly it can provide power for fridges for vaccines, and for lighting and TV, and it is clearly better environmentally than using a diesel generator. However, some critics see PV as too expensive at present for widespread use in poor countries, and argue that only when and if costs are reduced, by development and deployment in the industrial countries, can PV be usefully deployed on a wide scale elsewhere.

Inevitably, the success and appropriateness of a technology like PV will depend on the context. For example, in semi-desert areas, PV-powered water pumps for irrigation and water supply from wells may be the best option. Nevertheless, it is sometimes argued that for the moment, in much of the developing world, the use of biomass, small-scale hydro and possibly small-scale wind turbines makes more sense (Karekezi, 2002).

Technology transfer has to be carried out sensitively and effectively. For example, local people are often left to manage new energy systems, like PV arrays, which have been set up by western technical workers. If the local technicians do not have the expertise to carry out necessary maintenance, the system may fall into disrepair and be abandoned. This type of outcome highlights the need for technology transfer to cover skills transfer as well as hardware transfer, to build up the local technical infrastructure. The technical knowledge may then provide the basis for the local development of technologies and associated enterprises.

Technology transfer is not always a one-way flow. While poverty and lack of economic growth are widespread, not all developing countries are the same. Some are developing economically and technologically very rapidly. Their expansion is often based initially on imported technology, but as the developing countries establish their own industrial and export capacity they may develop their own technologies. Countries like China are rapidly becoming major players, and are offering technologies it has developed itself, for example solar PV, to developing countries.

Either way, technology transfer is a rapidly expanding area of activity, especially as markets and trade become increasingly global. Of course most transfer is not done for altruistic purposes. Companies in the industrialised world are looking for lucrative new markets for their wares. In some situations there is the risk they will dump inappropriate technology on developing countries, such as technologies that cannot be used in developed countries due to their stricter environmental controls. Certainly there can be problems with the uncontrolled diffusion of technology, and there is clearly a need for regulation. If global environmental problems are to be avoided, there may be a need for carefully selected transfer of clean and green technologies from the industrialised world, backed up by funding and educational programmes.

This is not the place for a full exploration of the role of technology transfer in regional and global economic development. There are plenty of texts on that issue if you are interested (see, for example, Wilkins, 2002). However, it is worth looking briefly at the more general question of whether efforts like this are likely to succeed in terms of enabling the developing world to avoid making major environmental impacts as they industrialise. Will they adopt the new green technological pattern? Will the newly developing countries become 'green tigers', competing with the developed world for the global green market? Or are most developing countries so poor they will need aid to avoid the worst eco-choices as they strain to just keep up?

Some environmentalists fear the emergent 'new' economies of Asia – China and India especially – will simply adopt the same environmentally unsustainable approach to industrialisation as was pioneered in the west. Others are cheered by the fact that India is now one of the world's leading countries in terms of using wind power – in 2004 it was fourth in the world wind power league – with nearly 2000 MW installed, and plans to put 10 000 MW of renewable capacity in place by 2012.

China has an even more ambitious renewable energy programme – it already has around 23 000 MW of solar heat supply capacity, large wind and biogas programmes and over 50 000 small hydro projects, as well as a large hydro programme, its largest renewable resource. Taken together, its use of these sources put it at number two in the 2002 world renewables generation league – only just being beaten by the USA. Brazil was number three, due to its large hydro programme.

Moreover, the potential for expansion of renewables in China is large and it could soon become the world leader. China's overall renewable energy resource has been put at around 400 000 MW and by 2020 it hopes to have around 20 000 MW of wind generation installed and 120 000 MW of renewables capacity altogether. This would meet around 12 per cent of its expected electricity requirements by that time. In 2005 it adopted a version of the REFIT approach to support the rapid development of renewables.

However, both China and India are also keen on nuclear expansion, and China's rapid economic expansion has been, and seems likely to continue to be, heavily reliant on its large coal reserves. There are ways in which the emissions from coal plants can be captured and stored, at a price. This is one of the aims of the new Asian–Pacific pact mentioned earlier. But longer term, the big issue is whether the renewables option will be followed up seriously.

As this brief look at China indicates, many uncertainties remain about the future pattern of energy provision. These uncertainties open up large issues, well beyond the range of this course, but they clearly relate to the way technology is developed, the pattern of technological diffusion and, crucially, who shapes it. This brings me back to the idea that users and consumers might be able to play a useful role in ensuring that appropriate technologies are developed and widely deployed.

SAQ 11

What are the problems with adopting a top-down approach to technology transfer in developing countries? Would a bottom-up approach be more relevant?

9.5   Conclusion

The global renewable resource is huge. A report by the German government for the major international Renewable Energy Conference held in Bonn in 2004 estimated that by 2050 renewables could be supplying 50 per cent of total world energy, not just electricity. However, to get to that level will require much more successful and widespread diffusion.

The imposition of technology through a top-down approach may lead to inappropriate and unsustainable solutions. In the next section you will look back at the bottom-up approach discussed in earlier sections to see whether that offers more opportunities for success.

Key points of Section 9

- Attempts are being made globally to stimulate the take-up of new greener energy technologies by creating emissions credit trading markets, based on the extra certificates that companies who reduce their emissions below specified levels can accrue.

- The carbon emissions trading concept may lead to the installation of cleaner technologies in developing countries, but the technology transfer process needs to be sensitive to the local context.

- Top-down approaches to innovation and diffusion may not be effective in supporting technology transfer to developing countries, or subsequent sustainable development.

The key points for Section 9 meet learning outcome 1.5.

10 Technological transitions and niche management

This section brings the discussion in this block to a conclusion by looking at some of the ways in which companies and governments are trying to make use of some of the more novel bottom-up ideas and techniques for stimulating diffusion discussed earlier.

10.1 Strategic niche management

Previous sections have shown that new products face problems gaining a share of the market because existing products dominate the market, backed by powerful companies with vested interests in maintaining their market share. In this situation it is not surprising that some new products emerge in marginal and sometimes obscure niche markets, where consumers and users can sometimes play a key role in the innovation and diffusion process.

While some products remain in their niches, others transcend their initial niches and become mainstream products. Previous sections have shown some examples of consumers and users developing products that have then diffused more widely.

10.1.1 Lessons from the past

Certainly, looking more broadly, there is no shortage of historical examples of niche developments that have expanded to lead to major changes. Adrian Smith (2003) suggests the emphasis should be on stimulating diversity and variety generation, followed by selection from successful developments – the approach recommended by Douthwaite.

> Historical research into the past transformation of some mainstream systems of technological practices, such as the move from sail power to steam power, the rise of the automobile, or the spread of telephones, indicates that the transforming technology and practice gained momentum through a series of niche applications, often on the margins of the mainstream. The niche applications are less sensitive to the higher costs and troubled performance of the promising technology. In part, this can be because the niche application overcomes a problem particular to that niche ... or it delivers something that is especially valued by individuals involved in the niche [so it is worth the extra expense or inconvenience]. This could include the ideals of those people, such as a desire to live more sustainably. As the niche performance improves with experience and learning, so more people are attracted to the technology. We get a move from idealists to entrepreneurs, who can see the business promise. The size of lead markets widens, and the range of applications is adapted, the original niche grows and new niches are created or branch off. Commercialisation gets underway and, if successful and with more experience, serious investment starts pouring in and mainstreaming takes place.
>
> ...

Not all niches succeed of course. Those that do often tap into wider changes or pressures in society and facilitate them further – such as growing mobility, or an ageing population, or environmental stresses or community needs. Precisely because it is not always clear which niche will succeed, some variety creation is important initially. In this way, with experience and learning we can select between the evolving niches subject to performance pressures.

Source: Smith (2003)

10.1.2 Protective environment for ideas

Interestingly, governments and corporate interests have become increasingly eager to see if they can tap into this niche development concept, by trying to identify and then support niche products in the hope of being able to stimulate the wider diffusion of strategically important new technologies. The approach is called strategic niche management. It involves providing a protected environment for selected new product ideas.

strategic niche management

an approach to diffusion that distorts normal economic pressures to allow a new technology time for development within a protected market

Clearly not every product idea is going to be a success, and there is a risk that protecting products from commercial pressures for a while may keep ideas alive that should have been selected out. However, there can be great benefits from nurturing the germ of an idea to give it a chance to develop.

10.2 Technological regime change and disruptive technologies

The advocates of strategic niche management argue for the creation of protected environments for new ideas. However, they also see a need to change the market context, as new technology is unlikely to prosper outside the niche until the market context has changed. Market change may involve little more than a shift in public awareness, so that a new product is seen as desirable. However, if the new technology is a major innovation, its widespread diffusion may require a much more radical change.

Strategic niche management theorists suggest the success of radically new products often requires a change in the underlying technological rationale, which is the set of assumptions about how technology is used and which technology is appropriate. These assumptions are usually reflected in the institutional and economic arrangements and infrastructures that have grown up to support the existing pattern of technological use – what the strategic niche management analysts call the current technological regime. Technological regime change is seen as necessary to enable radically new technologies to flourish.

technological regime change

a change in the underlying social, economic and institutional support arrangements associated with the adoption of a radical technology

For example, in the energy market the existing technological regime is based on the use of finite reserves of fuel, providing concentrated energy from a few large, centralised power stations that feed into national power grids. Major corporate and economic interests and institutions have emerged to sustain this pattern of operation and the support infrastructure. The energy system required for renewable energy technologies is much more decentralised, with power generation being carried out in larger numbers of smaller power plants dispersed around the country, often using local energy sources to meet local needs.

Instead of trying to promote renewable energy technologies to fit into the existing system, it is seen as more effective to present them as part of a new energy system. That means calling for a transition to a new technological regime and the development of new support infrastructure. It can also be argued that a new institutional regime would be needed because many of the organisations that grew based on the existing technologies will have to change to accommodate the new approach.

Transitions of this kind are not easy and take time, but they are often necessary before major new technologies can prosper. For example, when the motor car was developed, new roads, filling stations and infrastructure were developed over a long period. This eventually enabled motor transport to become dominant. The switch to a new transport infrastructure, for example based on the use of hydrogen as a vehicle fuel, would similarly take a long time to develop.

Of course, not every innovation demands a new technological and institutional order, but radically new technologies do tend to be associated with radically new ways of doing things. This is seen in the social and institutional changes that have occurred because of the diffusion of personal computers and information technology. A shift from reliance on large expensive mainframe computers run by large corporations and institutions, to the local use and ownership of small, cheap personal computers, effectively decentralised the technology.

10.2.1 Disruptive technologies

The concept of technological regime change has some overlap with the idea of radical technological change and discontinuities, which was discussed in relation to s-curve analysis in Section 1. S-curves can be used to depict how new technologies take over from older ones. However, as you may recall, there the emphasis was on technological changes within the same 'family' of product types and market sector (see Figure 4). Usually the changes depicted by s-curves do not require major social and institutional adjustments. In contrast, a technological regime change is likely to require major changes, and possibly major discontinuities and disruptions.

The *Invention and innovation* block discussed what Clayton Christensen calls *disruptive innovations*. His concept of technological change also has some similarities to the idea of regime change. Christensen argues that disruptive technologies require change in patterns of consumer use and institutional regime change in the wider world. In addition such technologies are also disruptive for companies, which may have to change their approach to marketing, and possibly their whole technology strategy. Initially though, he notes that the new technologies may only appeal to a limited number of people. Christensen argues that disruptive technologies 'have features that a few fringe (and generally new) consumers value'. So he also is talking about initial niche markets as well as subsequent regime change.

This has implications for how companies fund the development of such products and then market them. Christensen (2003) notes that disruptive products based on disruptive technologies usually offer lower profits and are most often developed as commercial products in emerging or insignificant markets. He goes on to say:

> By and large, a disruptive technology is initially embraced by the least profitable customers in a market. Hence, most companies with a practiced discipline of listening to their best customers and identifying new products that promise greater profitability and growth are rarely able to build a case for investing in disruptive technologies until it is too late. [Also] small markets don't solve the growth needs of large companies. The larger and more successful an organization becomes, the weaker the argument that emerging markets can remain useful engines for growth.

Christensen suggests that smaller companies are often in a better position to explore small niche markets, and recommends that large companies set up smaller subsidiary companies, or internal ventures, to do this if they want to stay ahead of the field.

In general, Christensen's analysis has much in common with the niche management approach, though he is more concerned with corporate commercial success, while the strategic niche management analysts are usually more concerned with wider economic, environmental and social issues related to technological change. Certainly, the changes implied by the strategic niche management concept of regime change are more radical than the disruptions described by Christensen.

Nevertheless, from a company or consumer perspective, the changes brought by disruptive technologies can feel as radical as a regime change. For example, the shift from large mainframe computers to the widespread use of small personal computers was a radical change. This led to a lot of infrastructure changes and presented a major challenge to mainframe companies like IBM that had dominated the computer market. After the change, consumers now have their own personal computers. However a new institutional framework emerged. The all-important software market is now dominated by one company, Microsoft, and the manufacturers Intel and AMD dominate the microprocessor market. In Christensen's terms, to put it simply, the disruption led one dominant company to be replaced by another. Whether this amounts to a regime change is a matter for debate.

A more recent development has been the rise in the use of the internet to download music and video. One of the growth areas is peer-to-peer file sharing which, despite being technically illegal, rapidly became popular with large numbers of people. Enthusiasts see tangible benefits from easy access cost-free entertainment. However, most research shows that file sharing has had a detrimental effect on the sales of CDs. Sharing large digital files in this way has only become possible on a large scale due to technical advances such as broadband.

This example shows how the advent of new technologies can disrupt existing trading and operational patterns, which in turn may threaten the existing corporate structures. The response of some companies to this trend was to develop services where music could be downloaded legally using micro-payment systems. Some companies, like iTunes, offer one free single a week to users of their software, and now allow anyone to upload and download pod-casts (radio programmes) for free, which encourages the use of the software interface and its related hardware (iPod, iNano and Apple computers). So, as Christensen suggests, an initial shock in the market may lead to new commercial opportunities.

While the advent of the internet and personal computers may arguably be part of a wider information and communication technology regime change, the development of downloadable music systems is not a regime change, though it is a disruption. However, it is clear the changeover from large centralised fossil and nuclear power plants to smaller renewable energy projects does involve a significant technological regime change. New technologies are required with new patterns of deployment and, initially at least, new companies to develop them, along with new ways of thinking about energy.

A radical technological regime change will also be needed in relation to transport systems to reduce the scale of climate change. There is little doubt that major changes in infrastructure-related systems like energy and transport would be full-scale technological regime changes.

SAQ 12

How does the idea of disruptive technologies relate to the idea of regime change? How radical do the technological and social disruptions have to be to amount to a regime change?

10.3 Sustainable innovation?

As some of the examples just cited suggest, the strategic niche management and regime change approach could in principle be applied in any technological and market context. But most strategic niche management analysts focus on the need to support the development of environmentally appropriate technologies, as part of a process of moving toward an environmentally sustainable future. The analysts seek to identify and support relevant niche developments. While these analysts recognise that not all niche products come from grass-roots initiatives, many subscribe to the view that bottom-up approaches are likely to be more successful than top-down approaches. This has led some to look at grass-roots initiatives of the sort I've described as possible starting points for what might be called sustainable innovations.

10.3.1 Grass-roots innovation and sustainable development

In a workshop session on 'Grass-roots Innovation and Sustainable Development' held in 2003, Adrian Smith argued:

> Sustainable innovations must include devising new ways of organising and carrying out activities that permit the penetration of more sustainable technological practice into the mainstream, that is, system building. There does not appear to be a shortage of green or socially useful ideas or technologies – PV, composting units, electric vehicles, and the list goes on – the shortage appears to be innovative routes to their widespread adoption.

The problem Smith identified is that adoption by the market may require social adaptation, such as changes in lifestyles. Niche developments, with their close involvement of users and consumers, are seen as an important way to 'pilot' the changes. These pilot uses of the new technology involve end-users closely in the refinement of the technology. However, the pilot projects are more concerned with developing a system of practice. So, for example, researchers have studied how pilot projects concerning electric vehicles in towns could be redesigned to make better use of participants' experiences. The pilot projects have looked at such questions as:

- Which types of people are prepared to make what kinds of lifestyle adaptation in order to use the new vehicle?

- What technical improvements are needed to the car in order to make it more attractive?

- How might a better electricity infrastructure be built to make it easier to recharge the vehicles?

- What policy changes or subsidies would move the vehicles closer to a commercial market?

- How can people start to think about their mobility needs differently?

- Which organisations possess the functions and resources (finance, authority, motivation, etc.) needed to bring about some of these changes?

The idea is that through creating and monitoring niches, effective changes can be put in place that will help the niche activity to become mainstream practice.

Smith concluded,

> What is interesting is that some researchers are advocating the deliberate creation of sustainable niches as experiments which will help seed more widespread transformations ... could grass-roots activity become one route for making sustainable technological practices normal, routine, even humdrum?

> (Smith, 2003)

10.3.2 Sustainable innovation projects with a social purpose

The term sustainable innovation is rather imprecise. What is meant is the development of technologies that will help support an environmentally sustainable approach to human activities. In reality, that may require much more than just technical change. The social use of technologies may also have to change.

It is a chicken-and-egg situation. Must society and the market context be changed before new technologies can be adopted widely, or can society just adapt to technology? The advocates of strategic niche management argue that it should be a two-way interaction. Ideally, they say, the role of those trying to support diffusion should be to enable the co-evolution of technology and markets. That means they should grow together, reinforcing each other. However, they recognise the pace of technological and market change may not be the same. Often the technology comes first, and its development is constrained by the slower development of the necessary infrastructure. To prepare the way for environmentally sound technologies it may be necessary to make changes in the wider infrastructure first.

So, for example, in the case of new energy technologies, rather than trying to bolster up the old centralised system, governments should support the development of new energy transmission and storage technology to allow the more decentralised and dispersed renewable energy sources to be used more effectively. In parallel, government should support and protect specific niche developments. This means not only new technologies but also social experiments with new ways of using technology such as community level experiments in the use of renewable energy that pioneer new approaches.

Several examples already exist, such as the long-established Centre for Alternative Technology in Wales, and the more recent Hockerton housing project in Nottinghamshire, and Earth Balance centre in Northumbria. All of these projects have demonstrated the viability of novel energy innovations of various kinds. As well as developing and displaying new technical ideas, centres like this can act as demonstration centres for new ideas about the way technology should be used, that is, ideas about appropriate lifestyles and sustainable consumption patterns.

The T307 DVD includes a section on the Hockerton housing project and some other green housing projects (see *Block 4 Guide*).

Bringing the idea of supporting community-orientated niche developments closer to everyday life, it is interesting that in 2003 the UK government launched a £10 million Clear Skies community energy programme, designed to encourage homeowners, schools and communities across the UK to take the initiative in developing and installing their own renewable energy schemes. The Clear Skies initiative was seen as a vital component of the government's renewables strategy to capture the imagination of individuals and local communities that wanted to play their part in the renewables revolution. Launching the scheme, energy minister Brian Wilson said, 'Renewable energy can be about thinking small as well as big. The Clear Skies initiative is an excellent opportunity for community groups and homeowners to bring forward useful projects.'

Most of the emphasis in grant-aided programmes like this and those that followed[1] is on deploying established technology in community settings with a strong social orientation. However, such schemes can help the diffusion of new ideas and practices and build the market for the new technologies. There may also be opportunities for product or system innovation.

10.4 Supporting diffusion: social acceptance

As you saw in the case of the local wind co-operatives in Denmark, community involvement can help to build local acceptance of and support for renewable energy projects, and this ensures wider

[1] In 2006 the Clear Skies scheme was combined with a new low-carbon building programme, which included £50 million support for microgeneration technologies.

diffusion. Direct local involvement can lead to a participative process that decides which projects are acceptable and which are not. More generally there is a need to develop a consensus on how to balance the global environmental benefits of renewables with the smaller, but usually unwelcome, local impacts.

Local involvement can provide a useful context for that debate. Given that local opposition to some projects has proved to be a key problem facing the UK renewable energy programme, it is understandable that the government launched community-orientated schemes like Clear Skies, as well as new planning rules requiring local councils to develop local and regional plans and targets for renewable energy (PPS 22, 2003).

Local community support will certainly be needed if the UK is to attain its target of obtaining 10 per cent of its electricity from renewable sources by 2010. The government estimated that up to £6 billion would be needed from the private sector to achieve this target. As noted earlier, the government itself is only providing relatively small amounts of funding directly, mostly in the form of grants for specific programmes. However, it is not surprising that some of these are geared specifically for community-orientated projects.

For a sustainable future to be socially equitable the necessary technological innovations must be publicly acceptable. Public hostility to change can block or at least slow down the adoption of innovations, as was seen with the public resistance to GM food in the UK in the late 1990s. Renewable energy technology is seen by some as a more attractive option that is less likely to be opposed than nuclear power plants are. But no technology can be entirely benign; there will always be some impacts and some opposition. Community involvement provides one way to try to avoid or reduce opposition and create the context for successful diffusion, as well as possibly opening up positive opportunities for bottom-up innovation.

Community initiatives can operate at various levels. So far this block has focused on grass-roots groups and individual enthusiasts. However, some interesting community-orientated energy initiatives have also been launched at local authority level. The following case study outlines an example in which a local council has successfully introduced an autonomous independent energy system for some of its residents. Energy is supplied not by the national grid but by what has been labelled a private wire scheme, fed by power plants run by the council. It has evidently proved to be popular locally not least because it delivers energy at less cost than the conventional system, while at the same time helping to reduce environmental emissions.

Case study Woking's private-wire community CHP

Woking Borough Council has a commitment to promoting energy efficiency and other environmental polices. Not only does it have an ambitious energy conservation programme for the properties it owns, but it has also developed the first private-wire combined heat and power (CHP) system in the UK. The council has adopted what is called an energy services approach – providing electricity, heat *and* energy conservation services rather than just supplying energy. Moreover, it has done this in an innovative way.

The private wire concept is particularly interesting and unusual. Consumers get their electricity from the council, not from the local regional electricity company. They also get their heat direct from the council by means of district heating pipe networks. For example, a gas-fired CHP plant provides cheap heating, hot water and electricity direct to residents of the council's sheltered housing sites.

The council's website explains that:

> To ensure that the council's investment is paid back, electricity and heat are sold at a higher value to residents than the price which could have been obtained by exporting it to the local regional electricity company. However, residents benefit because the price they have to pay is still lower than the normal domestic rate. This means that they make substantial savings on their energy bills with up to £120 each year off fuel bills for a one bedroom flat. At the same time, the CHP energy efficient technology is good news for the environment, saving an estimated 500 tonnes of CO_2 from being sent into the atmosphere each year.
>
> ...
>
> There has been 100% take up by residents in the housing where the scheme has been introduced.

The council's power network also covers other users, with, for example, a CHP plant supplying heat and electricity to civic offices and hotels in the city centre, and electricity from PV solar installations is also integrated into the network. In 2003 the peak generating capacity of the PV installations was 0.5 megawatt and the council claimed that Woking had the largest concentration of PV capacity in the UK. The council also installed the first commercial fuel cell in the UK, a 200-kilowatt unit located in Woking Park, fuelled by natural gas. It provides heat and electricity for the council's swimming pool and power for the park's lighting. Some of the heat is used to power the pool's air conditioning, cooling and dehumidification requirements, via a novel heat-fired, absorption cooling unit.

Although the system's various consumers get their power from the network, not from the national grid, there are grid links to the main plants on the network for back up. However, in theory, by using its various independent power inputs, the network could run independently of the national grid. As it can match local loads well, and avoid long distance power transmission losses, the system is claimed to be more efficient than the conventional grid system, and to have led to significant emission savings. The longer-term aim is to increase the amount of renewable energy used in line with the council's policy of reducing Woking's carbon dioxide emissions in steps of 10 per cent each decade up to 2050 and then 5 per cent per decade, with the ultimate goal being an 80 per cent reduction from 1990 levels by 2080.

Clearly the council has adopted a visionary approach, and is backing it up with a strong commitment to technological innovation. The approach taken to funding the ambitious programme was also innovative. It has been underpinned by the creation of a recyclable fund, topped up by financial savings achieved by the energy efficiency projects. The initial £250 000 allocated to the fund, together with grants from various government schemes, and savings from the energy efficiency programme, have allowed the council to provide £2.8 million in investment for new projects.

There was some organisational and institutional innovation. To take the programme forward, the council, in partnership with private sector companies, set up a joint venture energy services company, Thameswey Energy Limited. This company aims to 'design, build, finance and operate small scale CHP stations, fuel cells and other sustainable and renewable energy systems to provide energy services by private wire and distributed heating and cooling networks to institutional, commercial and residential customers'.

Other local councils have shown an interest in the ideas pioneered by Woking, and in 2004, the originator of the scheme, Woking's energy manager Allan Jones, was appointed by the Greater London Authority to oversee London's climate change response programme.

The DVD contains a video looking at the Woking initiative (see *Block 4 Guide*).

10.5 System innovation and regime change

The Woking initiative opens up a range of issues: for example, can a local council help its residents to opt out of the national power system? Technically it seems that it is possible, and perhaps even advantageous. It has also provided a context in which the latest environmentally sound energy systems could be employed. So this initiative seems to be technologically innovative and to have aided the adoption of new ideas that have been able to develop in the niche context provided by the council. However, it involved more than just the adoption of a few new individual technologies – it integrated them, as well as new operational and organisational practices, into an innovative system, so it can be seen as an example of system level innovation.

This sort of development is larger scale than most of the grass-roots initiatives you have looked at in this block, which have in the main, at least initially, involved a few individuals or small groups. While smaller scale initiatives can, cumulatively, play a role in diffusing new technologies and practices, it is likely that if larger, system-level, niche developments are successful and widely adopted, they could play a more significant role in bringing about a transition to a new technological regime.

The Woking initiative certainly prefigures a shift to a more decentralised, and arguably more sustainable, energy system, which might be taken up more widely.

It does seem, however, that with larger projects like this, there is less opportunity for direct local involvement – the Woking initiative was a municipal project introduced and managed on behalf of local people but only involving them as users, albeit users who have some influence on the council's activity via local democratic processes. Nevertheless, a lower level of local involvement may not be inevitable with such projects. For example, the innovative renewable energy system developed by local residents on the Danish island of Samsø (see the T307 DVD video) is almost on the same scale as Woking, and many local people were involved with setting it up.

Those interested in promoting sustainable approaches will obviously want to ensure that large-scale system-level initiatives like this are widely adopted as part of a process of transition to a new technological regime. However, there is still much debate about exactly what the driving force behind such transitions is, and therefore how they might best be stimulated. You have looked at the practicalities of how appropriate specific projects can be supported, for example via targeted funding to stimulate diffusion and the involvement of consumers and users. But there is the wider issue of what drives overall changes and transitions of this type.

There is no shortage of theories on this issue, some of them being quite sophisticated in terms of trying to apply recent theories of 'evolutionary economics' and 'emergent system behaviour' to the study of technological change and sustainable development (Boelie et al., 2004). As the theorists point out, there are many possible causes of change, and possible points of intervention by those wishing to support change, some based primarily on economic models of change, others on technological factors.

Some theorists argue there are cyclic patterns of innovation, possibly driven by economic trading cycles, with regular waves of new technologies emerging to form the basis of new technological regimes. This is sometimes called long-wave theory. Other theorists, however, suggest that social and cultural factors play an important role, if only in mediating changes caused by other factors. For example, it is sometimes argued that technological changes will not be viable until the necessary social and attitudinal changes have occurred, and these social changes can often take longer than technological change.

The reality is probably that all these factors interact in complex, dynamic ways, at various stages of the innovation process. This block has stressed the need to involve consumers in the innovation process, partly to ensure that emerging new technologies are accepted. But consumers' involvement can only be part of a larger process of change – there are larger forces at work. Some theorists argue that large-scale technological transitions only occur when the continued economic viability of the existing technological regime has become exhausted or blocked in some way. Resource scarcity, for instance running out of oil, would be an example of a major reason for change; environmental constraints, for instance climate change problems, on the continued use of fossil fuels would be another.

Certainly there is a transition to a new technological regime, with, arguably, renewable energy technology being one candidate for a disruptive technology that is emerging as part of this transition. In which case, although they may only have a small role, some of the niche developments described in this block could provide a useful starting point, not least in creating the new attitudes needed for the wider transition to be successful.

10.6 Conclusions and wider applications

This block has focused mainly on renewable energy projects, but of course the idea that bottom-up initiatives can help wide acceptance and diffusion of novel ideas and practices is relevant in many other areas.

Another example of the role of bottom-up initiatives is found in the area of energy efficiency and conservation. Much of the initial progress made on energy conservation was led by grass-roots activists conducting practical, hands-on campaigns, often with a strong social and community element, making use of well-established techniques, for example setting up voluntary teams to insulate elderly people's houses. There is now a whole range of off-the-shelf technologies that reduce energy wastes, and a national network of energy-efficiency advice centres overseen by the Energy Saving Trust, as well as many local voluntary groups.

Energy conservation is crucial in all sectors of the economy, and there are many opportunities to develop clever energy saving innovations. There are also many ways in which existing energy efficient technologies and practices can be more widely diffused. Although government funding has proved to be vital, as has the support of local authorities, the successful diffusion of energy efficiency initiatives in the domestic sector clearly benefits from a grass-roots approach to delivery.

The widespread acceptance and adoption of domestic waste recycling was also to some extent due to the pioneering work of many local voluntary groups and community-orientated campaigns and initiatives. Self-help initiatives also play a role in the diffusion of ideas, and such initiatives have led to the growing acceptance of such things as organic food, car-share schemes and community-based wireless broadband for rural areas.

As these examples indicate, the social and organisational side of the initiative is often as important as the technology, in terms of gaining acceptance, achieving operational success and stimulating diffusion. These examples also highlight the fact that many sustainable innovations concern system-level changes – that is, an interaction between technologies and social networks, rather than just isolated gadgets used by individuals. In addition, the emphasis is on systems that deliver services to consumers, which may require system-level innovation.

An example might be the idea of energy companies shifting away from the provision of just electricity to consumers and on to offering complete energy services, heat, power and support for the efficient use of these services. Consumers want warm rooms and power for electrical equipment, not electricity or gas as such. As you have seen, this energy services approach was one element in the Woking initiative, delivered by the development of an innovative community-scaled energy system. The *Consumption* block looks at this type of innovation in more detail.

Exercise 6   Community support

This block has looked at some examples of situations where community support was vital for the successful diffusion of new technologies and was obtained by the direct involvement of local people, in some cases as consumers and users, or even developers of the technology – as in the case of wind projects in Denmark. Can you think of examples where it would be hard to obtain this sort of grass-roots involvement and therefore perhaps difficult to get popular support for diffusion?

Discussion

The degree of local support for projects seems to come down to:

- an assessment of the balance of local costs versus local benefits
- the opportunity for niche market development and/or local level entrepreneurial involvement.

Therefore wind projects were popular in Denmark because local people could benefit financially from them by being members of local wind co-operatives, with some even being involved with the development of the technology, whereas this was not the case in the UK.

In some cases it may be possible to win local support for an unpopular technology by offering cash inducements, for example grants for building a local swimming pool, or some other form of compensation. This approach has been suggested as one way to win support from local communities for the location of nuclear waste repositories or toxic waste dumps in their area. But it can seem like bribery.

Otherwise unattractive and unpopular projects may offer some compensation by bringing employment and other economic gains to the local area. The benefits of nuclear power plants are sometimes portrayed in this way. But it is hard to see how local people can be involved more directly with projects like this – there is little opportunity for direct community ownership. The same limitations apply to many other large-scale industrial, civil engineering and infrastructure projects – such as airports and motorways.

But it is not just a question of scale. If there are problems and uncertainties with the technology and these are seen as having an impact locally, then opposition is likely whatever the scale, as the resistance to GM crops in the UK, locally and nationally, shows. Rightly or wrongly, this technology was seen as being imposed on an unwilling public, with no opportunity for involvement and no identifiable benefits, just risks.

Local perceptions are of course not always right. They are inevitably, to some degree, parochial and partisan. There may be wider frameworks to consider, nationally and internationally, which could change the assessment. That seems to be why wind power attracts overwhelming support in UK national opinion polls, in the context of a response to global climate change, but is sometimes resisted at local level due to perceived local disbenefits. In contrast, nuclear power and GM crops seem to be generally unpopular with the public at both levels.

There is also no shortage of examples of grass-roots initiatives that have failed. But then again there are also plenty of examples of top-down projects that have failed – the initial UK and US wind turbine development programmes, for example, with their emphasis on large machines.

Clearly, in addition to debates about the validity or otherwise of grass-roots views and interpretations, there is plenty of scope for disagreements about the viability or need for bottom-up grass-roots approaches, as well of course as plenty of examples of failure of top-down approaches. Hopefully this block will have given you some benchmarks and examples that can help you come to your own conclusions.

Key points of Section 10

- New product ideas can sometimes emerge in niche markets, possibly via bottom-up grass-roots initiatives in response to specific social needs or environmental concerns.

- It may be possible to stimulate the development and wider diffusion of successful new products by supporting them in the earliest stages of development to allow bottom-up incremental adjustment and improvement, before the products leave the niche.

- This strategic niche management approach may lead to disruptive new technologies that cannot be accommodated within the existing technological and corporate framework: radical new products may require a changed context in order to prosper.

- Grass-roots initiatives may not only lead to the bottom-up development of new technologies, but can also provide a context in which new patterns of sustainable social use of technologies can be developed and accepted.

- For a sustainable future, the emphasis in innovation may need to shift from products to systems and services, with new patterns of social use being important.

The key points for Section 10 meet learning outcomes 1.8 and 1.9.

11 Conclusion

This block has reviewed a range of approaches that are used to manage the diffusion of new technologies, using renewable energy technology as the main example. You have seen some of the approaches to the diffusion of new green energy technologies used by governments, and read the arguments about why reliance on short-term market considerations may not be the best way to support the development of technologies that address longer-term environmental problems. It was also argued that top-down approaches to innovation and diffusion are not always appropriate. You have also looked at the extent to which users and consumers can influence the way technology is developed and diffused.

This final section reviews and rounds off the discussion by revisiting some of the key themes covered in the block, the main one being the contrast between top-down industrial and corporate approaches and bottom-up independent and community approaches to innovation and diffusion.

11.1 Industrial involvement

You have already read that many companies have branched out into the green technologies. What seems to be happening is that as novel ideas for green products emerge and begin to look commercially interesting, they are taken up by large companies. However, many large companies have major innovation programmes of their own. For example, some of the more advanced renewable energy technologies owe their existence to the work of large high-tech companies. In recent years, companies like Shell and BP have invested in renewables, like photovoltaic solar, and have major support programmes for rapid diffusion. Some of the energy supply companies have made similar investments.

In the wider market beyond energy technologies, many companies of a range of sizes are investing in the development of environmental products.

It is clear that large companies must play a major role if the transition to a sustainable future is to be achieved. However, for the successful diffusion of the new technologies and the development of new ways of thinking about how technology is used, there is also a need for the involvement of a wide range of people and communities. Quite apart from any positive contribution they may be able to make to innovation, wider public involvement is important as a way to help ensure the new technologies are diffused in acceptable ways.

11.2 Community involvement

The case of wind farms in Denmark shows how local involvement by communities and local businesses helps to smooth the way for the acceptance of what might initially be seen as unfamiliar and threatening new technologies (Figure 28). A spokesperson for one of the leading UK green power retail companies summed up the situation well.

Without consumers, both individuals and businesses, making decisions on the way energy is planned for, developed and used, the whole shift to the brave new world will not be sustainable. ...The new paradigm of a carbon free energy world will need to involve people and business in planning, developing and implementing renewable energy. Some of the key barriers to implementing a renewable energy solution are due to its 'decentralised' low intensity nature, and as such there will be no option but to implement these solutions near where we live and work. Without the acceptance and the encouragement of individuals and businesses, the success of this type of development on the scale that is necessary is unlikely. In short, actively empowering individuals in the decision making process to develop renewable energy must be key to the success of the strategy.

(Davenport, 2003, p. 9)

Figure 28   Local residents turn up to watch the first of three 1.3-megawatt turbines being erected on the locally owned Moel Moelogan wind farm in Wales in 2003

In 2002 the UK government launched a £1.6 million Community Renewables initiative, which was subsequently run in parallel with the £10 million Clear Skies programme mentioned earlier. This initiative aimed to help schools, offices and housing developments play a part in reducing the effects of climate change. It had an additional aim not only of creating environmentally friendly developments but also enabling community groups to benefit directly from any income generated, for example through the generation of local employment by the creation of new enterprises and community-based projects.

The UK government has also taken a number of initiatives to increase public awareness by running campaigns focused on the practical action consumers can take. For example, in the early 2000s the UK government ran an 'Are you doing your bit?' campaign aimed at stimulating people to take environmental problems and practical solutions to them seriously. The government also launched a campaign called 'It's only natural' to alert consumers and others to the benefits of renewable energy. Environmental issues have also become a part of the school curriculum.

As well as government-supported initiatives, there are many grass-roots groups promoting green technologies and trying to stimulate grass-roots discussions about sustainable consumption, technology and lifestyle changes. Consumers may eventually reach a state of awareness where new greener products and technologies diffuse more widely, and they may even want to have more say about what is developed and even, in some cases, initiate projects themselves. However, it is a long way from self-help initiatives and community enterprises to major corporate programmes of product development and diffusion.

11.2.1 Grass-roots initiatives

A conference on 'Grass-roots Innovations for Sustainable Development' held in 2005 defined grass-roots initiatives as follows:

> Grass-roots initiatives are innovative networks of activists and organisations that lead bottom-up solutions for sustainable development; solutions that respond to the local situation and the interests and values of the communities involved. In contrast to conventional, incremental green reforms, grass-roots initiatives seek to practice deeper, alternative forms of sustainable development.

> The initiatives involve committed activists who often seek to experiment with social innovations as well as using greener technologies and techniques in areas such as housing, renewable energy, food, and alternative money. They frequently seek to create new social institutions and 'systems of provision' based upon different values to those of the mainstream. Examples include community renewable energy initiatives, ecohousing, local organic food schemes, and community currencies such as time banks.

(Renew, 2005)

The innovations created by grass-roots groups can sometime create lucrative new markets, but such success can present problems. While wide diffusion may be perceived as beneficial, the grass-roots initiators might not be happy with losing control of the process. The innovators may be concerned that some of the initial ideas might be corrupted by being shorn of their community-orientated social values. Grass-roots groups might end up just providing the ideas or the contexts for schemes they help to pioneer and test, but that are then taken over by powerful agencies, exploiting and co-opting grass-roots enthusiasm.

You will be looking at how some grass-roots groups have developed ideas for sustainable living and sustainable technology in the *Consumption* block. But one thing is clear, they tend to have radical ideas, often going beyond just products and on to wider services and systems, and they also often develop different ways of using them. Many grass-roots groups have their own ways of operating, and they may not be happy to lose their independence. So there could be potential conflicts if local schemes or programmes are being seen as being imposed and manipulated by outside interests.

One delegate at the grass-roots conference commented, 'We don't want grass-roots groups to just participate passively in other people's research projects – they should be innovators not guinea pigs.'

The bottom-up approach may not possible in every situation. In some cases, the technical expertise and technological requirement may be beyond the reach of all but those employed by large well-financed organisations. But this problem can be overstated – it may not apply in all situations. As you will recall, Box 4 looked at an example of a bottom-up process that led to the creation and diffusion of computer software by an informal and independent network of computer experts, Linux. To some extent it could be that the advent of advanced communication and computer systems has made it possible for most people to get involved with the innovation and diffusion process if they want to.

Exercise 7   Bottom-up approaches to innovation

Can you think of some areas of technology where a bottom-up approach to innovation and diffusion may not be viable?

Discussion

Actually it is not that easy to find examples of impossible areas – there are nearly always some niches. But here is my attempt. Your list may differ.

Advanced high-tech aerospace projects – the preserve of large companies like Boeing and specialist agencies like NASA. However, there are many semi-amateur aircraft enthusiasts, including model plane enthusiasts, some of whom develop novel ideas. There are also some independent space launcher projects – one (the Starchaser) even being promoted by an OU graduate.

White goods – high volume products clearly require large organisations, but in some cases the initial product idea can still come from more humble beginnings, as James Dyson illustrated with his vacuum cleaner and Trevor Baylis showed with his clockwork radio.

Vehicles – again high-volume products like cars are the forte of large companies, but some novel ideas have emerged from other sources, especially for new types of bicycles, where sports enthusiasts can play a role. The boating and yachting world also has its share of enthusiastic innovators.

Military weapons projects – unfortunately, some so-called rogue states, or even terrorist groups, may not see working independently of the major defence companies on advanced weapons systems as a problem.

Large civil engineering projects – some buildings can involve innovative designs, based on vernacular and incremental approaches. But large-scale projects tend to be unremittingly top-down. Nuclear power also seems to fit in here.

To summarise, the bottom-up approach may not be possible in every context, but where it is viable it seems to succeed because it adopts different product selection criteria and associated social values from the top-down approach. Maybe, as companies expand their ethical and environmental concerns, the top-down and bottom-up approaches will come together.

SAQ 13

Innovation increasingly involves technically sophisticated engineering. Does that mean that grass-roots involvement by non-experts must inevitably be a marginal activity?

11.3 Consumer and corporate responses

To round off this block, let me go back to the factors that Rogers says influence the diffusion of new products. You should recall that these factors are *relative advantage, compatibility, trialability, observability* and *complexity*. I also might add *perceived risk* or *danger*.

Let me consider how these factors might shape consumers' reactions to new energy technologies at the domestic level, like PV solar on rooftops, or fuel cells in homes delivering electricity and heat.

You may recall that Exercise 1 asked you to look at consumers' responses to mobile phones and the general conclusion was that this technology scored highly on most counts. Mobile phones are familiar items with a high degree of perceived utility. In contrast, the new energy systems are much less observable and trialable, and some can be quite complex to install and maintain. Most consumers are indifferent to how electricity is supplied – it just comes out of the socket.

These technologies may eventually become more familiar if they are adopted by companies and local government to meet their energy targets. Some consumers may see little relative advantage in adopting these technologies, especially as the cost of installation is high, but they may eventually conclude that there is an environmental advantage. Other consumers may find the technologies interesting and desirable. In the latter group there will be those who are strongly committed to this change for environmental reasons and others who are technological hobbyists and enthusiasts, some of whom may be pioneers in adopting, promoting and possibly even developing the new technologies. That group may be small, but it could have a large impact on innovation and diffusion.

On the issue of perceived risk, some may see self-generation, for example by PV on the roof, as risky as well as complex in terms of providing reliable energy supplies. But some might see it as a way to be less at risk from the potential failure of grid supplies.

A further example of reaction to new technological options is the diffusion of new products from a corporate perspective. In his book *The Innovator's Dilemma*, Christensen (1997) provides a case study of the way in which companies have positioned themselves in relation to the new technology of electric vehicles. He sees electric vehicles as classic disruptive technology and describes how companies have decided to focus on niche markets; for example, some families may use them as second vehicles for local shopping or as suitable vehicles for teenage leisure use. You may be able to think of other possible niches.

Since Christensen wrote this case study, most automobile companies in the USA have decided to abandon the battery-electric vehicle market in preference for cars with hybrid engines and more advanced hydrogen-based technology. For example, in 2002 Ford decided to abandon the

Think electric car, the battery powered vehicle concept it had bought in from a small company in Norway in 1999 for $23 million. This was due to 'poor customer demand' and 'lack of government support for the environmentally friendly cars'. Ford spent $100m on new battery technology, but felt this was not the way forward. Instead, in common with most other auto makers, it is focusing on hydrogen fuel cell and hybrid gasoline-electric vehicles. Toyota and Honda had already developed hybrid petrol–electric cars (the Honda Insight and Toyota Prius) while BMW had developed a hydrogen-powered car, which burns hydrogen in a conventional engine. More advanced, DaimlerChrysler has the fuel-cell-powered NeCar5, which has a methanol-to-hydrogen chemical reformer on board.

Although it was generally agreed that fuel cell cars were some years from a commercial launch, a new technological trajectory opened up. This was consolidated in 2003 by the announcement by President George Bush of $1.7 billion national commitment over five years 'to take hydrogen fuel cell cars from the laboratory to the showroom'. It will be interesting to see if this top-down approach is successful. Certainly, a regime change on this scale is likely to require more than bottom-up initiatives.

You could also say the same about the wider shift to a sustainable energy system based on renewable energy technology. It will take major social and economic changes, as well as a major technical transition, to change to a system in which greenhouse gas emissions are reduced by 60 per cent – as is the UK government's current commitment – by the year 2050. Realistically, given the technological, institutional and financial resources required, and the need for global level action, there will be a need for both bottom-up and top-down initiatives to bring about this sort of transition, especially if it has to be attempted within a few decades.

That could stand as the final general conclusion of this block. Given the complexity and cost of technology, for successful innovation and particularly for successful diffusion, you may need both a top-down and bottom-up approach, although which, if any, should dominate will depend on the context and the technology.

11.4 Sustainable consumption?

This block has focused on the potential role of consumers and users in shaping the innovation and diffusion process, mainly in the context of the development and spread of sustainable energy technologies. It seems reasonable to ask if the role of the consumer can be more than just a passive market-based one where their voice is heard only through their purchasing decisions.

Given the growing concern about a range of environmental and social issues related to the impact of technology, it does not seem unreasonable for consumers to play a more positive and active role in shaping what emerges. It may be true that active ethical and environmental concern is only apparent in a minority of consumers and some alert companies. However, the debate on the idea of moving towards what has been called sustainable consumption seems bound to grow, as will pressure for new approaches to choosing and developing appropriate technologies (Figure 29).

Figure 29   Buying green products may be only half the story – sustainable consumption may also require changes in lifestyle

Innovation is often seen as central to economic growth, but perhaps the real issue is whether there is something called sustainable innovation. While some innovations can clearly cause environmental problems, others can help solve them. Is it possible to shift the balance to the latter? Or is the problem larger than that, and to do with the drive towards ever-increasing levels of consumption? If so, then the key issue is can technological innovation allow consumption to continue to grow without undermining the environmental life support system? If not, can it help to develop more sustainable lifestyles and consumption patterns? The next block picks up these issues, rounding off the course by asking you, in effect, to consider the question, can innovation support a move to sustainable living?

> To draw together some of the themes from the final part of this block and as a preparation for the next block, look at the following final two exercises.

Exercise 8   Influence of consumer power

This block has argued that consumer power could provide a new influence on the innovation and diffusion process. Looking back over the examples of bottom-up initiatives provided, review whether you think this is realistic or not, and whether they indicate the emergence of new types of consumer orientation.

Discussion

To some extent this is a matter of debate – there are no right or wrong answers. However, this block has provided what are hopefully some interesting examples of cases where grass-roots initiatives of various kinds have led to new or modified products, and in some cases to new markets. Whether they represent a significant new trend is harder to say. You might also ask whether this trend is related to consumers. Isn't it more to do with grass-roots enthusiasts, inventors and those with special interests, preoccupations and needs? However, once a minority of users of some special product or service – who may also have had a hand in creating it – has expanded out of a niche market, and has become a majority, then the resultant community of users is in effect a conventional consumer market. To put it simply, consumer support is obviously necessary for the successful diffusion of products, and that is true for niche products.

Exercise 9   Carbon offset schemes

A UK-based organisation called Climate Care is offering to offset the emissions people make using energy at home or when driving or flying by investing in a range of carbon saving or avoiding projects, including renewable energy generation (small hydro upgrade projects), rainforest restoration (for carbon sequestration) and energy conservation projects (supplying low-energy light bulbs to communities in the developing world). They have teamed up with the Environmental Transport Association (ETA) to offer special packages. For example, the ETA says the 350 kg of CO_2 emitted by a typical car over 1000 miles could be offset by a payment of £2.75, and your 125 kg share of the emissions produced by one hour of flying for £1. You can also offset your typical annual domestic gas and electricity related emissions (5 tonnes) for £40, and the total 'average British citizen's annual emissions' (11.3 tonnes) for £90. The ETA is even offering to offset the 20 kg emitted per recovery by its vehicle breakdown service for £1 per recovery.

Does this sort of scheme help consumers to influence the way technology is used and which technologies are used?

Discussion

This sort of scheme certainly allows consumers collectively to influence some types of decision and, if taken up widely, could shape some patterns of investment, but it is a fairly indirect form of influence, even more indirect, arguably, than the various green power tariff schemes discussed earlier (Section 3). The cynical view may be that what is being offered by the likes of Climate Care is guilt-free consumption. However, it is also true that such schemes can help offset emissions that lead to climate change, so they do offer an opportunity for altruistic and ethical engagement by consumers.

Of course you might also say that avoiding or minimising the emission-related activity directly yourself would show even more commitment. That of course would mean either changing lifestyle or changing technology, or possibly both. The interaction between consumption and technological innovation and their impact on sustainability is the topic of the *Consumption* block.

SAQ 14

Innovation and diffusion are arguably mainly the concerns of companies and government. How can consumers play a useful role in support of diffusion and innovation?

SAQ 15

As indicated in the *Markets* block and the *Products* block, in the case of the multinational company Philips, engagement with users was seen as important for successful innovation and diffusion. The company took great pains to study consumer reactions and needs. What extra lessons have emerged from the discussion in this block concerning the practical consumer-orientated steps that can be taken by innovators working in companies to promote the successful diffusion of new products?

SAQ 16

This block has looked at some bottom-up approaches, which innovation theorists like Boru Douthwaite see as effective in some areas of innovation. I have given examples of consumer-initiated innovation and diffusion often based initially on niche markets. How does this approach compare with the approach adopted by Christensen, which was looked at in Section 10 and in the *Invention and innovation* block?

SAQ 17

In terms of the discussion of technology push and market pull in the *Invention and innovation* block, how would you classify the bottom-up grass-roots initiatives looked at in this block?

SAQ 18

Why has this block, which is ostensibly on diffusion, often looked beyond diffusion and looked at the wider innovation process?

Key points of Section 11

- New technologies are needed to help respond to a range of environmental problems.

- Industry and government have a major role to play in the development and diffusion of such technologies, a top-down approach.

- Consumer and community involvement in the innovation and diffusion process may also be needed to ensure that new more sustainable technologies are developed and accepted.

- There are many opportunities for innovative bottom-up approaches, but there will also be a need for top-down approaches in order to move towards a sustainable future.

- Technological solutions on their own may not be sufficient. There may need to be a change in the pattern of the social use of technology and a shift to sustainable consumption.

The key points for Section 11 meet learning outcomes 2.1, 2.2, 3.1 and 3.2.

Answers to self-assessment questions

SAQ 1

Proactive consumers are a minority, a small group of altruistic enthusiasts with special interests of little significance to mainstream markets. So why bother to consider this marginal group in any detail?

It is true that most people are passive consumers, selecting from what is on offer. But, as was suggested in Section 1, increasingly consumers are becoming more selective in relation to health, ethical and environmental issues. This is beginning to feed back into the innovation process as companies become aware of changes in market response, viewing 'innovators' and early adopters as the first in an expanding market for green or ethical products. Although the numbers may be relatively small, there are cases where consumers get directly involved with innovation, and in some sectors this may have a major influence on the development of both the technology and the market.

SAQ 2

What factors might limit the rate of take up of green power tariff schemes by UK domestic consumers?

1 Many consumers do not know about the schemes. In the UK they have not been widely advertised because the supply companies were worried that there would not be sufficient green power supplies to meet demand if it grew too rapidly.

2 Not all consumers are concerned or know about the environmental impacts of using conventional energy sources.

3 Consumers may think the process of changing suppliers will be difficult.

4 If the schemes involve a premium price, that may put all but the most altruistic consumer off.

SAQ 3

What advantages did the grass-roots Austrian solar collector innovators have over conventional corporate innovators?

The grass-roots enthusiasts had much lower overheads; they were working on a voluntary basis, not charging for any expertise they might have. The device itself was also better suited to most users because it had gone through a process of developmental testing by users, with DIY in mind. The technology that emerged had an immediate market in the network they had created and the goodwill they engendered helped to ensure sales via word-of-mouth reputation, so they did not need expensive marketing or advertising.

SAQ 4

In terms of Rogers' classification of types of adopters as outlined in Section 1, how did the Austrian solar collector innovators differ from the energy consumers in California who adopted PV solar?

Solar PV has been adopted by some people already in the USA, so the Californian consumers were perhaps late adopters, helping to continue and widen the diffusion process. The Austrian consumers who developed solar collectors were 'innovators', both in technological terms although it was an easier technology to develop, and also in terms of the way their initiatives led to diffusion of the technology in the market.

SAQ 5

To what extent did any of the examples of proactive consumer initiatives discussed so far involve radical product invention?

Only the wind turbine initiative in Denmark could be seen as truly innovative in technological terms, and even that was derived from existing windmill designs. The Austrian solar collector projects were even more straightforward adaptations of existing concepts. In most cases this seems to be the pattern – consumers adapt what is on offer, and only occasionally do novel ideas emerge.

What distinguishes the proactive consumer initiatives looked at in the block from low-level adaptation approaches is that they also created a new market, that is, they were proactive in terms of diffusion.

SAQ 6

Innovations created by proactive consumers are a rare thing. Isn't most innovation carried out by large teams in companies?

It is true that not many consumers are proactive and even fewer develop their own ideas for new products or systems. But then innovation is itself an activity only carried out by a relatively small number of people. As you will recall from the *Invention and innovation* block, innovation is mainly carried out in large companies, but as Section 6 illustrates there is still an important role for individuals, including those outside the corporate context.

So highly motivated enthusiasts and dissatisfied consumers can be a source of new ideas, some of which may succeed and diffuse widely. And in some sectors, for example computer software, this can be a major influence.

SAQ 7

In terms of the various stages of the innovation process, from invention through to diffusion, how has the focus of the *funding* provided by the UK government for renewable energy changed from the 1970s onwards?

Initially R&D funding was provided to researchers in universities, government laboratories and company laboratories – a technology-push approach. This was followed by a market enablement approach, first the NFFO and then the Renewables Obligation, targeted at energy supply companies, with the emphasis being on creating a competitive impetus for the adoption of renewable energy. However, some extra subsidies in the form of grants had to be allocated to developers to make this approach work in the case of some of the newer less commercially mature technologies, and some grant money has also been allocated to new start-up initiatives and enterprises.

SAQ 8

Given that it is difficult to pick winners in terms of identifying areas likely to be worth investing in for innovative effort, why should the government try? Why not leave it up to the private sector and the market to decide?

It could just be left to the private sector and investors, and ultimately, the market, to decide which options are likely to be most commercially viable. The trouble with this is that it means the focus tends to be on the short term and investors are often averse to risk and may avoid novel ideas even though these projects may be needed for strategic reasons in the longer term.

SAQ 9

What do you think is the explanation for the linear nature of log-log learning curves? Why does a straight line emerge covering *all* the various stages of innovation?

It seems reasonable to assume that at the early stage of a product's development, the rate of innovation will be high, a lot of improvements being made on the original prototype designs. Subsequently, as and when, and if, the product reaches the market, further rounds of improvement may occur, in response to operational experience and user feedback. And then later, if the product sells well, there are economies of scale in volume production that can produce price reductions and there will usually be further incremental performance improvements.

So, on an ordinary performance (for example pence/kWh) versus time curve, you might expect an initial rapid improvement, as rapid technical improvements are made on the original prototype. On a product volume (for example kW installed) versus time graph, you might expect a slow start, followed by rapid and continuing improvement as the product goes to mass production. Combining these and transferring to a log-log performance versus volume graph, the result is usually an overall straight line.

SAQ 10

In the 'Selecting energy options for the UK' case study in Section 8, the Carbon Trust outlined the conditions under which it might be worth the UK getting into renewables. How does its analysis compare with the views of Chase, as quoted above?

The Carbon Trust seem rather hesitant about recommending action unless there are clear environmental and economic gains, and ideally the economic gains should include both domestic sales *and* export potential. Otherwise the UK might just import the technology, or do nothing. Chase by contrast is somewhat more bullish, although he seems to agree. He suggests that for some countries there could be much to gain by being first in with renewables, but he doesn't say which countries.

SAQ 11

What are the problems with adopting a top-down approach to technology transfer in developing countries? Would a bottom-up approach be more relevant?

Section 9 suggested that in some cases top-down approaches were ineffective because the technologies were not suited to the context, and sometimes could not be used or maintained effectively. It was argued that bottom-up initiatives might help match the technology more effectively to the local context and help local people to develop the necessary skills for operation and maintenance and a capacity for indigenous innovation.

SAQ 12

How does the idea of disruptive technologies relate to the idea of regime change? How radical do the technological and social disruptions have to be to amount to a regime change?

Some new technologies may need social and institutional changes before they can be widely used – so they are disruptive to the status quo, and certainly they can challenge the existing technologies, and the markets in which they have been operating. Clearly, as Clayton Christensen has argued, disruptive technologies of various types can present challenges to many existing companies. But the scale and impact of the changes involved with regime changes are arguably often of a different order that suggests radically new patterns of technology and associated institutional and corporate arrangements and infrastructure.

SAQ 13

Innovation increasingly involves technically sophisticated engineering. Does that mean that grass-roots involvement by non-experts must inevitably be a marginal activity?

Not necessarily. Although some technologies preclude amateur involvement – nuclear power is an obvious example but there are many more – there are also many that might benefit from a fresh perspective. Looking back over the examples of grass-roots projects provided earlier in this block, the level of technical expertise varies. In some cases professional level expertise was involved (for instance Linux) and certainly craft-level inputs and insights can often prove valuable, as was indicated in the Danish wind power example.

In addition to any technical input, community and consumer inputs can also ensure the technology that emerges is socially acceptable and appropriate to users' needs. That is vital for successful diffusion.

SAQ 14

Innovation and diffusion are arguably mainly the concerns of companies and government. How can consumers play a useful role in support of diffusion and innovation?

It is true that most innovations are the result of efforts by companies to develop products that will sell to consumers, with governments perhaps providing support for specific lines of development deemed strategically important. However, as has been argued in this block, the diffusion process can be greatly aided if consumers and users are involved in some way. Indeed, motivated consumers and users can sometimes create markets for new areas of innovation.

Even when it comes to just responding to innovations developed by others, the social and community context is important for diffusion. Certainly diffusion may be delayed or prevented if the community opposes the innovation – as was illustrated in the case of wind power.

More positively, bottom-up initiatives from the grass-roots can sometimes throw up original ideas that can be diffused widely. Indeed, in some sectors this can be a major source of innovation in terms of new product development, as well as aiding diffusion.

SAQ 15

As indicated in the *Markets* and the *Products* blocks, in the case of the multinational company Philips, engagement with users was seen as important for successful innovation and diffusion. The company took great pains to study consumer reactions and needs. What extra lessons have emerged from the discussion in this block concerning the practical consumer-orientated steps that can be taken by innovators working in companies to promote the successful diffusion of new products?

Philips clearly researched consumer reactions and needs. However, this block has gone further and looked at examples where consumers have become proactive, sometimes developing their own ideas, and creating niche markets. From the corporate innovator's point of view, there could be much to be gained by linking into this process because it can identify new trends and needs, and even sometimes offer new technologies. Options for engagement might include setting up two-way dialogues with local enthusiasts on newly emergent ideas, supporting pilot projects and niche initiatives. However, while providing technical support to them might be welcomed, there could also be suspicions that your company was trying to absorb the ideas and exploit the market.

SAQ 16

This block has looked at some bottom-up approaches, which innovation theorists like Boru Douthwaite see as effective in some areas of innovation. I have given examples of consumer-initiated innovation and diffusion often based initially on niche markets. How does this approach compare with the approach adopted by Christensen, which was looked at in Section 10 and in the *Invention and innovation* block?

Christensen's 'disruptive technologies' sometimes emerge from niche markets created by fringe groups. Douthwaite suggested that consumers with special requirements, initially perhaps only representing niche markets, are the potential drivers for new products. So in this respect there is not too much difference in the approaches. However, the tone, style and, possibly, the motivation seem to differ. Christensen is more concerned with corporate concerns and proposes top-down managerial approaches. Douthwaite is more concerned with getting new socially and environmentally appropriate technologies established and focuses on bottom-up approaches.

SAQ 17

In terms of the discussion of technology push and market pull in the *Invention and innovation* block, how would you classify the bottom-up grass-roots initiatives looked at in this block?

The proactive consumer and user initiatives looked at in this block seem to rely on a non-commercial type of market-pull effect operating initially within a niche market that reflects local needs and requirements. But there can also be an element of technology push, as the initial impetus may rely on enthusiasm for specific technologies as a way of resolving the problems or meeting the needs that have been identified by users and consumers.

SAQ 18

Why has this block, which is ostensibly on diffusion, often looked beyond diffusion and looked at the wider innovation process?

At the simplest level, there cannot be any diffusion unless a successful product has been developed. More subtly, feedback mechanisms between diffusion and product development are important for successful innovation. Indeed, in the initial phase of some of the cases of grass-roots innovation initiatives looked at in this block, the product development and diffusion processes are directly linked or even indistinguishable – it is users and consumers who are doing the product development. It has been claimed that this close interaction can lead to novel and successful developments. To varying degrees, some companies have also recognised the need to link into niche developments.

Even in the case of large-scale innovation programmes supported by governments, user and consumer involvement is important for success. In fact, for some novel technologies, positive support from consumers may be vital if they are to succeed and those consumers may want a say in what is developed and how it is deployed. So there are continuing interactions between each phase of the innovation process.

References and further reading

Agar, J. (2003) *Constant Touch*, Duxford, Icon Books.

Austrian Academy of Sciences (1996) *Express Path*, report.

Bechberger, M. and Reiche, D. (2005) 'Europe banks on fixed tariffs', *New Energy*, no. 2, April.

Boelie, E., Geels, F. and Green, K. (2004) *System Innovation and the Transition to Sustainability*, Cheltenham, Edward Elgar.

Boyle, G., Everett, B. and Ramage, J. (2003) *Energy Systems and Sustainability*, Oxford, OUP and Open University.

Butler, L. and Neuhoff, K. (2004) *Comparison of Feed in Tariff, Quota and Auction Mechanisms to Support Wind Power Development*, report from the University of Cambridge Department of Applied Economics; also available online at ideas.repec.org/p/cam/camdae/0503.html#abstract (accessed January 2006).

Carbon Trust (2003) *Building Options for UK Renewable Energy*, report, London, Carbon Trust.

Carbon Trust (2004) *Renewables Innovation Review*, London, Carbon Trust/DTI.

Cellular Online (2006) data available online at www.cellular.co.za (accessed 5/5/06).

Chase, R. (1998) 'Climate change – a role for business', Speech at the Royal Institute of International Affairs, London, November.

Christensen, C. M. (2003) *The Innovator's Dilemma: The Revolutionary Book That Will Change the Way You do Business*, New York, HarperCollins (first published 1997).

Davenport, J. (2003) 'Energy policy has to be supported by people', *PowerHouse*, PRASEG, March, p. 9.

Douthwaite, B. (2002a) *Enabling Innovation*, London, Zed Publications.

Douthwaite, B. (2002b). 'How to enable innovation', *Agricultural Engineering International: the CIGR Journal of Scientific Research and Development*, vol. IV, October, pp. 7–8.

Economist (1996) 'Being digital is not enough', Technology Brief, *The Economist*, 28th September, p. 142.

Elert, G. (2003) The Physics Hypertextbook, [online] hypertextbook.com/facts (accessed 19/4/2006)

Elliott, D. (2003) *Energy, Society and Environment*, London, Routledge.

Fischer, C. (2004) 'Who uses innovative energy technologies, when, and why? The case of fuel cell micro-CHP', *Transformation and Innovation in Power Systems*, Berlin, Forschungsstelle für Umweltpolitik, Freie Universität Berlin.

Fischer, C. (2005) 'From consumers to operators: the role of micro-CHP users' in Pehnt, M. et al., *Micro Cogeneration: Towards Decentralized Energy Systems*, Berlin, Springer.

Green Electricity (online) www.greenelectricity.org (accessed 28/4/06).

Greenpeace (online) xs2.greenpeace.org/~ozone/greenfreeze (accessed 21/4/06)

Grotz, C. and Fouquet, D. (2005) 'Fixed prices work better', *New Energy*, no. 2, April.

Hödl, R. and Plesch, R. (1988) 'Fünf Jahre Solaranlagenbau – Eine Erfolgsbilanz', *energie info*, 1/88, p. 8.

Holdsworth, M. (2003) *Green Choice: What Choice?* London, National Consumer Council.

IEA (2000) *Experience Curves for Energy Technology Policy,* London, International Energy Agency, OECD.

International Telecommunication Union (2005) data available online at www.itu.int/home (accessed 24/11/05).

Karekezi, S. (2002) 'The case for de-emphasizing PV in renewable energy strategies in rural Africa', paper to the World Renewable Energy Congress, Cologne, June 29–July 5. Contact: African Energy Policy Research Network.

Kristensson, P., Gustafsson, A. and Archer, T. (2004) 'Harnessing the creative potential among users', *Journal of Product Innovation Management*, vol. 21, pp. 4–14; also available online at userinnovation.mit.edu/papers/Kristensson.pdf (accessed 4/5/06).

Leadbeater, C. (2005) 'Design your own revolution', *The Observer*, 19 June.

LogicaCMG, 2004

Luthje, C. (2004) 'Characteristics of innovating users in a consumer goods field', *Technovation*, vol. 24, pp. 683–95.

Mokyr, J. (1990) *The Lever of Riches: Technological Creativity and Economic Progress*, Oxford University Press.

Morris, D. (2001) *Seeing the Light: Regaining Control of our Electricity System*, Minneapolis, Institute for Self Reliance.

NAO (2005) *Renewable Energy*, London, National Audit Office: see their consultants OXERA's review *Renewables Support Policies in Selected Countries*.

NATTA (2002) *Greening Electricity*, Milton Keynes, Network for Alternative Technology and Technology Assessment.

Ornetzeder, M. (2001) 'Old technology and social innovations: inside the Austrian success-story on solar water heaters', *Technology Analysis & Strategic Management*, vol. 13, no. 1, pp. 269–78.

Papanek, V. (1972) *Design for the Real World*, London, Thames and Hudson.

PIU (2001a) *Technical and Economic Potential of Renewable Energy Generating Technologies: Potentials and Cost Reductions to 2020*, Working Paper 'h' produced for the energy review carried out by the Cabinet Office Performance and Innovation Unit; also available online at www.number10.gov.uk/files/pdf/PIUh.pdf (accessed January 2006).

PIU (2001b) *The Economics of Nuclear Power*, Working paper produced for the energy review carried out by the Cabinet Office Performance and Innovation Unit; also available online at www.number10.gov.uk/files/pdf/PIUi.pdf (accessed January 2006).

PPS 22 (2003) *Consultation on Draft New Planning Policy Statement 22 (Renewable Energy)*, London, Office of the Deputy Prime Minister.

Raymond, E. S. (1997) *The Cathedral and the Bazaar,* (online) available at www.catb.org/~esr/writings/cathedral-bazaar/cathedral-bazaar (accessed 3/4/2006).

Recording Industry Association of America (1997) *Annual Report*, RIAA; available online at www.resortrecords.com/downloads/RIAAdata.xls (accessed 5/5/06).

Renew (2005) 'Grassroots Innovations for Sustainable Development', (online), CSERGE, University of East Anglia and SPRU, University of Sussex, www.uea.ac.uk/~e175/grassroots.htm (accessed 4/5/06).

Rogers, E. M. (1983) *Diffusion of Innovations*, New York/London, Free Press; fourth edition 1995.

Ross, D. (2002) 'Scuppering the waves: how they tried to repel clean energy', *Science and Public Policy*, vol. 29, no. 1, pp. 25–35.

Select Committee (1984) *Energy RD&D in the UK*, House of Commons Select Committee on Energy, Session 1983–84, Ninth Report, London, HMSO.

Select Committee (1992) *Renewable Energy*, House of Commons Select Committee on Energy, Session 1991–92, Fourth Report, vol. III, March, London, HMSO.

Select Committee (2001) *Wave and Tidal Energy*, House of Commons Select Committee on Science and Technology, Session 2000–2001, Seventh Report, HC 291, April, London, HMSO.

Select Committee (2003) *Towards a Non-Carbon Fuel Economy: Research, Development and Demonstration*, House of Commons Select Committee on Science and Technology, Session 2002–03, Fourth Report, London, HMSO.

Smith, A. (2002) 'Transforming technological regimes for sustainable development: a role for appropriate technology niches?', paper 86, Science and Technology Policy Research, University of Sussex; also available online at www.sussex.ac.uk/Units/spru/publications/imprint/sewps/sewp86/sewp86.pdf (accessed 5/5/06).

Smith, A. (2003) Notes for a workshop on grass-roots innovation and sustainable development.

Sustainable Africa (2002) 'New mobile phone firm for January', (online) AllAfrica Global Media; available online at allafrica.com/sustainable/stories/200212110862.html (accessed 4/5/06).

Toke, D. (2005) 'Wind planning crisis – it's our fault' *Renew*, vol. 153, Jan–Feb. US Department of Energy, (2003) *Solar America*, CD-ROM.

WADE (2005) *World Survey of Decentralized Energy*, Edinburgh, World Alliance for Decentralized Energy.

Wilkins, G. (2002) *Technology Transfer for Renewable Energy: Overcoming Barriers in Developing Countries*, London, Earthscan.

WISE (2004) 'Finland: demo at Olkiluoto revives movement', *Nuclear Monitor*, vol. 615, World Information Service on Energy.

Acknowledgements

Grateful acknowledgement is made to the following sources:

Text

Pages 58–59: Fischer C. 'Who uses innovative energy technologies, when and why? The case of fuel cell MicroCHP', *Transformation and Innovation in Power Systems*, August 2004. Used with permission of the author.

Pages 124, 125, 128, 129: Smith, A. *Grassroots Innovation and Sustainable Development*, Presentation notes. June 2003. Adrian Smith, SPRU, University of Sussex.

Tables

Table 1: Hansard, November 21st 2001. Crown copyright, reproduced with permission from the Controller HMSO.

Figures

Figure 1: © Science and Society Picture Library.

Figure 5: RIAA (1997) *Annual Report: Technical Report*, 'Unit Sales of US Music Recording Media', Recording Industry Association of America.

Figure 6(a): Taken from www.privateline.com.

Figure 6(b): Courtesy Dr Martin Cooper, ArrayComm.

Figure 8: Courtesy of Aqualisa.

Figure 10: Solar Energy Technologies Program for US Department of Energy.

Figure 11: Courtesy of Susan Roaf.

Figure 12: Courtesy of Solarcentury.

Figure 13a: Courtesy of Onboard Energy.

Figure 13b: Courtesy of Microgen.

Figure 14: Copyright © Renewable Devices S.T. Ltd 2005.

Figure 15: Courtesy of West Wales Eco Centre.

Figures 17 and 18: Ornetzeder, M. 'Old Technology and Social Innovations: Inside the Austrian Success-Story on Solar Water Heaters', *Technology Analysis & Strategic Management*, Vol. 13, No. 1, 2001.

Figure 19: Elliott, D. (2003) Energy, Society and Environment, Routledge, Taylor & Francis Ltd. Copyright © 1997, 2003 David Elliott.

Figure 20: © Adam Schmedes/Lokefilm, www.lokefilm.dk.

Figure 22(a): Courtesy of The Engineering Business Ltd

Figure 22(b): Courtesy of Marine Current Turbines™ Ltd